PENTECOST BETWEEN BLACK AND WHITE

PENTECOST BETWEEN BLACK AND WHITE

Five case studies on Pentecost and Politics

WALTER J. HOLLENWEGER

CHRISTIAN JOURNALS LIMITED
BELFAST

First English edition 1974 by Christian Journals Limited, 2 Bristow Park, Belfast BT9 6TH.

Copyright © Christian Journals Ltd.

ISBN 0 904302 03 2

Cover by Blaise Levai
Typeset by Christian Journals Ltd.
and printed in Ireland by
Cahill & Co., Dublin

Contents

Preface

The 'theology of revolution' is silent on the freedom songs of the black people. It is as if these songs do not exist. 'Such silence is inexcusable.' James H. Cone, a black theologian from the United States, voiced this reproach. It is hard, he continued, not to conclude that many 'are enslaved by their own identity with the culture and history of their slave-masters'. Even if one discounts much of this sweeping statement, the fact is obvious that our debates on development policy, political theology, studies on 'Church and Society', 'theology of revolution', 'theology of liberation' or whatever may be the slogans, ignore some of the most revolutionary aspects of the newer enthusiastic movements of our time—such as the Kimbanguists in the Congo, the black Pentecostals in the United States and the Indian Pentecostals in Mexico.

I see the reason for this less in the prejudices of the respective theologians than in the difficulties of getting exact information on the socio-political and in fact revolutionary role of these movements. They belong mainly to an oral culture and what they have produced in print so far has not uncovered the real nature of their theology. It is only in these last few years that some of the Black Pentecostals (such as Leonard Lovett, Arthur Brazier and Morris Golder) have produced printed documents which

9

show something of the political and social dynamism of Pentecost. Even in my 'The Pentecostals' I could not concentrate sufficiently on this aspect, as I intended to give an overall picture of Pentecostalism.

I want to make up now for this lacuna. Two black, a brown and two white Pentecostal movements are presented in this book. All of them function more or less as religious and revolutionary catalysts of transformation in society. This statement is in contradiction to much that one generally hears about them. In order to make my point perhaps I have overstressed 'the other side' of these movements in this book.

I am particularly interested to show that in these movements there is a hitherto unexplored potential for real partnership between black and white, poor and rich, illiterates and intellectuals. Pentecost is that event which broke down the walls of the nations, colour, language, sex and social class. The oral, enthusiastic spirituality, Pentecost between black and white, is a potential medium of partnership, because the medium of the oral and narrative form is common in all the groups with which I deal in this book, independent of their other national, cultural or linguistic roots. In the context of Pentecost, partnership means that we, the white people, not only give but also receive, that we not only teach but also learn. It may well be that these black churches can offer models of thinking and communication which are perhaps not wholly unknown in the West but which are greatly 'underdeveloped'. The body of Christ can only come to its full maturity when all the gifts of all its members reach full interplay with each other. That such interplay has universal appeal was tested in practical experiments at the World Missionary Conference at Bangkok (1972/73) and also at the German Evangelical Kirchentag (1973). For the first time in church history a tough, but honest and humane, dialogue was possible between black and white in Bangkok.

'Between black and white' means furthermore that after previous denigration of enthusiasm we do not now just pass over to hallelujas. I do not want to hide the fact that in many cases Pentecostal spirituality obscures the real societal and structural relationships—but the same could be said to be true of mainline Protestant and Catholic spirituality. It would be unjust to make the theology of the reformation responsible for the social and political blindness of many Protestant churches. But it would be equally unjust to declare Pentecostal spirituality to be the root-cause for the a-political position of many Pentecostals. That this is not the case can be seen even in the Jesus People Movement (which is rightly seen as a response to the 'misère affective' in the affluent society). But even there one finds original and efficient political contributions.

One thing can be expected from Pentecostal spirituality. It replaces resignation by hope. And hope is something which many Christians today lack. There are many who are courageous. But they lack imagination, they lack 'ecstatic reason' which would give some content to their courage. There are others who have plenty of imagination but no courage. It is of course true that we need both. This book was written because I want to kindle hope, hope which has its roots in courageous imagination and is not afraid even of a 'phantastic' courage.

My secretary, Mrs. Joan Pearce, and the Reverend Wilbert Forker have helped to put my Swiss English into a more readable version of this beautiful but tricky language, for which they deserve my sincere thanks.

Birmingham, Pentecost 1974.   Walter J. Hollenweger.

I. A Kite Flies Against the Wind

Black Power and Pentecostalism in the United States

The United States 'must choose between democracy
and repression, between the republic and a police state;
for America cannot keep down thirty million people who
are moving up, without destroying the entire nation in the
process.' This was not written by a critical leftist theologian, but by a black Pentecostal evangelist in Chicago:
Arthur Brazier.

In an exact and detailed report he describes one of the
slum quarters of Chicago, the so-called Woodlawn. This
is not an idyllic park lawn but a slum area where 60,000
black people vegetate on two square miles in indescribable
conditions of hygiene, where garbage is either not, or only
partly, collected, where rats and vermin reign, and the
children learn so little in their over-crowded classes that
on leaving school they only swell the army of unemployed
and the drug-addicts.

Brazier protests against this state of affairs. He wants
to destroy the myth of the intellectual and moral suprem-
acy of the white. America, he says, was built on the backs
of the blacks. The blacks planted the cotton. But they
walked around in rags. The blacks built the railways. But
they were not allowed to ride on them. A black doctor

discovered blood plasma. But he died because nobody was ready to give him a blood transfusion.

Changing this situation cannot be effected by the violence of arms, but only by the violence of non-violence. We black people, he writes, we are also for law and order. But not for that law which the white wants to force upon us, a law which brands as criminals the demonstrators who publicize this appalling state, while those who are responsible for this situation are left in peace. We do not understand by law the practice of the police by which a suspect can be shot down as a criminal and which makes the policeman judge, juror and hangman in one person. Certainly, Brazier concedes, the majority of the police do not misuse their power. But there are too many who do.

How does this violence of non-violence work in practice? Brazier's programme consists in a programme of self-determination for the people of Woodlawn. It is called Woodlawn Organization. At the start it was subsidized by white churches but it is organized and directed by the blacks of the slum area. It is up to the blacks to do something themselves about the up-grading of their houses. Otherwise they will never learn to organize, to think and to co-operate. Under the direction of Brazier and other black Pentecostals, Woodlawn Organization sets up control-stations where those who feel that they have been cheated in the shops can check prices, quality and weight of the goods they have bought. Offending shop-keepers are taken to task and, in the case of repeated offenders, their names are published. House owners, who make their money in Woodlawn by over-charging on rents, but who themselves live in the villas of the suburbs, are informed of the miserable state of the houses they rent out, of the plague of rats and woodworm. But that hardly helps. So then the press and television are invited in to photograph the defunct toilets, the houses where the heating system has

14

ceased to function, the houses where the plaster is falling down, where the doors and windows are cracked and the roofs leak. This is uncomfortable for the owners but seldom alters their ways. Generally Woodlawn has to go a step further and has to organize a rent strike—the rents are paid to an account of Woodlawn Organization instead of to the bank of the owner. If the lazy house owners go to court, all their misbehaviour is exposed.

Similar programmes are invented for improving the miserable schools, which are under white direction. In order to put an end to looting and shooting—against which the police are almost powerless—two youth organizations ('Rangers' and 'Disciples') have been trained and used to maintain order.

Theologically these different activities are seen within the framework of a Pauline doctrine of charisms. In addition to the charisms which are known in the history of Pentecostalism, such as speaking in tongues, prophecy, religious dancing, prayer for the sick, they practise the gift of demonstrating, of organizing and publicizing as another kind of prophecy. I have met black Pentecostal churches in which these activities were explicitly mentioned in a list of gifts of the Spirit but not in the way in which it is usually done in many political church groups in Europe where political analysis replaces prayer and song (not to speak of dancing and speaking in tongues), but in forming a new unity between prayer and politics, social action and song.

The Black Pentecostals awake

In this battle the church is ahead of the world. That is how Brazier summarizes his book. Yet Brazier is not a unique example. During a research tour of the most important black Pentecostal churches in the USA (whose adherents number millions, I discovered similar programmes. Dietrich Bonhoeffer has already drawn attention

15

to these 'step-children of church history'. Yet their oral theology (which is handed down in the same way as, according to form criticism, the process took place in New Testament times before it was written down), their missionary work in the West Indies, their elementary social and political reflection is still ignored and even misunderstood as a preliminary form of fully-fledged European literary Christianity both by white Pentecostals and by the main-line churches. However, there are important exceptions, not so much in the standard works on social ethics, church history or histories of theological thought, but, for example, in the thoughtful study of worship by the Roman Catholic liturgiologist Lothar Zenetti, who has dedicated his book 'Hot melodies' to a black Pentecostal church (Temple Church of God in Christ), in whose midst he has experienced the power of the living Holy Spirit and the 'new song', or also in the travel report by Ernst Benz, professor at the university of Marburg, who describes in his book 'The Holy Ghost in America' his first encounter with black Pentecostals as a 'surprising discovery of something absolutely new', and not to forget the masterly 'Religious History of the American People' by S. E. Ahlstrom who gives some recognition to Black Pentecostalism.

An increasing awareness of the inherent values in black culture can be observed amongst the black Pentecostals. One of these black churches, the Church of God in Christ, claims to be the greatest Pentecostal church in the USA, in spite of the fact that hitherto the Assemblies of God has been considered the number one Pentecostal denomination in the United States. Yet the Church of God in Christ claims twice the membership of the white Assemblies of God. Another group, the Church of the Living God, has developed an interesting exegesis of the Bible by claiming that most of the Bible saints, including Jesus, belong to the black race. In a long discussion they

16

explained to me: As Jesus is descended from David and Abraham (both belonging to the black race), Jesus himself belongs to the black race. But at the same time, they added, we know that he did not have an earthly father. That is why he belongs to all men and not just to the blacks. He represents the whole of humanity.

Concerning social issues Bishop F. D. Washington, from the Church of God in Christ, deplores the church's 'mental block' which is responsible for a false understanding of evangelism because it attempts to promote the church building or organization when, as he states, 'whether we like to admit it or not, the church (as a building or denomination) has the poorest appeal of all to sinners. Its rating is exactly zero, because most sinners do not go to church. Yet the fantastic fact remains that the person of Jesus Christ—when He is presented right—has the greatest single appeal to the human heart in this world.'

It is only logical that this black Pentecostal leader was greatly attracted by the concept of evangelism as presented in the studies of the World Council of Churches. 'How can one join this World Council of Churches?', he asked abruptly and unexpectedly. It is furthermore understandable that the strike of sanitation workers in Memphis under the leadership of Dr. Martin Luther King had its headquarters in the big Mason Temple of the above-mentioned Church of God in Christ. The murder of Martin Luther King hit the black Pentecostals in a very personal way, but has so far not destroyed their hope in the power of non-violence.

But it means further that they cannot go along with a purely 'spiritual' evangelism. In an interview on Billy Graham the black Pentecostal evangelist George M. Perry said: 'We believe in the content of the Graham message, but we can't go along with its suburban, middle class white orientation that has nothing to say to the poor nor to the black people.' In short, mass evangelism practised by

17

the Reverend Billy Graham and other preachers—Perry concluded—never had and never will have any relevance to the black community.

'A theology developing out of any oppressive situation such as the black scene in America must begin with the socio-cultural factors that act upon one's humanity for good or evil', says the black Pentecostal theologian Leonard Lovett in an unpublished paper. And he adds: 'The avoidance of local problems of socio-economic injustices and discriminations in changing society on the part of early White Pentecostals led to what Fidler refers to as a "fatalistic Premillenialism which allowed White Pentecostals to relegate the close range problems to 'when Jesus comes', while in foreign areas they could 'rush the rapture' with a distant paternalistic application of Christian love and concern." '

Another issue which might be even more disturbing for the white Pentecostal denominations is the discovery by some researchers not only of the Afro-American, but also of some of the original African roots of the Pentecostal revival. But why should that frighten us? As God chose the despised children of Israel to bring blessings to the whole world, he chose again black slaves (including that which was good in their pagan past) to bring blessings to their white masters, to the church universal. After all, Christianity was not born in Europe!

Revolutionary past of white Pentecostals

It is clear that this new orientation of black Pentecostals is watched by the established white Pentecostal churches of the USA with uneasiness. However they know that they themselves trace back their history to a revival in a black church in Los Angeles (1906). The Pentecostal movement began in the same milieu in which the spiritual, jazz and blues emerged. Yet while black music has gained recognition as a contribution by the negroes to universal culture,

18

the black influence on the Pentecostal movement, which has today around thirty million adherents, has been forgotten in spite of the fact that in their books the Pentecostals mention the one-eyed black evangelist, W. J. Seymour, as one of their pioneers. 'That the one outstanding personality in bringing about the Pentecostal revival in Los Angeles was a Negro is a fact of extreme importance to Pentecostals of all races' states the young Pentecostal historian Vinson Synan. I agree with this evaluation even though one of the prominent white leaders of this early period, Charles F. Parham, was a convinced follower of the Ku Klux Klan, because Synan underlines the significance of the inter-racial nature of early Pentecostal revival. 'Even more significant is the fact that this inter-racial accord took place among the very groups that have traditionally been most at odds, the poor whites and the poor blacks.' Even more astonishing, white Pentecostals received their ordination from the hands of black Pentecostal bishops. A Pentecostal eye-witness, Frank Bartleman, proudly relates that, in the revival in Los Angeles which according to most Pentecostal authors is at the roots of the modern Pentecostal movement, 'the "colour line" was washed away in the blood'. Another Pentecostal pioneer, the Anglican clergyman Alexander A. Boddy, described the revival in Los Angeles to be 'something very extraordinary' because 'white pastors from the South were eagerly prepared to go to Los Angeles to the Negroes, to have fellowship with them and to receive through their prayers and intercessions the blessings of the Spirit. And it was still more wonderful that these white pastors went back to the South and reported to the members of their congregations that they had prayed in one Spirit and received the same blessings as they', a tradition which today is followed up by the neo-Pentecostal Anglican leader in Great Britain in a statement which was made explicitly against the British Conservative politician Enoch Powell: 'To deny a coloured person the same human rights as a white one, or treat a person differently because of the colour of his skin, is a sin against God. A prophetic ministry should seek to bring conviction of this sin to those who indulge in it.'

That last remark by Michael Harper might soon be tested out within the British churches. It is to be seen whether in future the very numerous and still growing Black Pentecostal Churches in Great Britain (some of them being of African but most being of West Indian origin) will find their way into the British Council of Churches and what that will mean for ecumenical and race relations in Britain. So far it is difficult to get precise information on the many and diverse Black Pentecostal Churches in Britain. They form the only Christian group in Britain which is growing amongst the black population in Britain. Roswith Gerloff, who is preparing a thorough study on Black Pentecostal Churches in Birmingham, holds that their social and theological contribution for the British churches and society as a whole is considerable. But that issue would have to be discussed on the basis of her research which has so far not been published.

Dare we think that the British Pentecostals and the British churches as a whole will do better than their American counterparts? For in America Pentecostals are strictly separated in white and black organizations, even though here and there one finds black pastors in subordinate posts in white organizations and the black Pentecostals usually appear at the Pentecostal World Conferences. Why has the originally integrated and inter-racial Pentecostal movement in the USA developed into a segregated church?

'No explanation has been offered as to why the Negro churches have not become part of the organization' of the Pentecostal Fellowship of North America. The reason for this development lies on the one hand in the loud criticism against Pentecostalism voiced by the main-line churches which tried to discredit Pentecostals by pointing to their lowly beginnings in a Negro church, and on the other hand in the laws of the Southern states of the USA which have prohibited racially mixed meetings. It would therefore be unfair to blame the white Pentecostals alone for this development. They have simply adapted themselves to what was considered at that time to be American Protestantism.

Black Pentecostals are not satisfied with the feeble attempts of white Pentecostals in America to understand social and political commitment as a task for the individual Christian (and not for the churches as a whole), and the very tardy and generalized appeals for Christian love of one's neighbour to be extended to the social field. For the black Pentecostals the 'Pentecostal problem' is the 'cleavage of the races', which must be solved before the movement can 'shake the world'. The appeal of the Assemblies of God for 'conversion', 'not coercion' will fall on deaf ears as long as it continues to be uttered only to those below and not equally loudly to those above.

One can understand the pastor of the Assemblies of God in Alabama who stated: 'I felt that the greatest indictment against the church of the Lord Jesus in our country is our stand (or lack of one) on racial problems.' And the historian of the Pentecostal Assemblies of the World, Morris E. Golder, compares the baptist Martin Luther King and his liberating ministry ('almost singlehandedly he challenged the mores of the South') to the high-flung statements of the Pentecostals on the power of the Holy Spirit. Golder says: 'If the white [Pentecostal] brethren would have stood firm against prejudice and racial injustice, having the most powerful authority (the Holy Spirit) and the most powerful message (the Gospel of Jesus Christ), they could have been the

21

instruments of God for the destruction of this hideous ideology. But instead of fighting against it, they submitted to its influence and have been affected by it even until now.' And Lovett concludes: 'Black Pentecostalism affirms with dogmatic insistence that liberation is always a consequence of the presence of the Spirit. Authentic liberation can never occur apart from genuine pentecostal encounter, and likewise, authentic pentecostal encounter cannot occur unless liberation becomes the consequence. It is another way of saying *no man can experience the fullness of the Spirit and be a bona fide racist.*' (Italics mine). I wonder what white Pentecostals have to say to this pneumatology!

The songs of the blacks

It has already been mentioned that the Pentecostal movement arose in the same milieu in which the today famous music and the songs of the blacks originated. Opinions vary concerning the origin and function of the Negro Spiritual. It is either considered as a misinterpreted hymn of the white Christians (G. P. Jackson), as a 'confession of faith' of the black church (S. Läuchli, Th. Lehmann), as the 'clearest exponent of the Negro's real self' (H. W. Odum), as an oral document of events in the history of the American Negro (M. M. Fisher), as a protest against social injustice (J. Lovell), as an adaptation of African songs (H. E. Krehbiel; Du Bois), as songs originating in the camp meetings of the white revival movement (B. T. Washington), as the products of black bards like 'singing Johnson' and 'Ma White' (J. W. Johnson), or as a blending of American and European melodies with African rhythm (E. M. von Hornbostel). Whatever the history of the Spiritual, it is the origin of at least four musical trends today: 1. The different styles of jazz including the Blues. 2. The music found today in white Pentecostal churches, which is rooted in black music but which has been greatly changed and adapted to the white ear, particularly in the USA where some of the earliest hymn writers were black Pentecostals. 3. The spontaneous gospel music which is more contemporary and related mainly to the Pentecostal churches and some black Baptist churches. The Gospel song is indigenous to the community within the church and reflects the current living conditions of the congregation in contrast to the more traditional Spiritual. 4. Attempts to adapt it to European and American traditional Church music. Yet there is great controversy as to whether the spiritual has a place in a non-black church service, a controversy which becomes even sharper when the Spirituals are translated into French or German or when they are sung in English by a non-English congregation.

Whether one accepts M. M. Fisher's interpretation of the Spiritual as a means of communicating historical data in an oral culture to save the black past from being forgotten, or not, it is certain that the Spiritual is a powerful means of communication which has 'preached' and communicated the Gospel in black American communities more powerfully than any book or sermon. And it is this element of Black spirituality that was taken up by the Pentecostal revival in those parts of the world where it was really successful, be it in Latin America, in Zaïre, in Italy, in Indonesia or in Russia. Where Pentecostals work in a pre- or post-literary society they do not think along systematic and logical lines but in parables and associations. Their main medium of communication is not the book or the newspaper but the proverb, the chorus, the joke, the testimony, the miracle story, the television and radio programme.

These songs are not, as James H. Cone pointed out, unpolitical and other-worldly. 'Contrary to popular opinion', says Cone, 'the spirituals are not evidence that black people reconciled themselves with human slavery. On the contrary, they are black freedom songs which

23

emphasize black liberation as consistent with divine revelation. For this reason, it is most appropriate for black people to sing them in this "new" age of Black Power. And if some people still regard spirituals as inconsistent with Black Power and Black Theology, that is because they have been misguided and the songs misinterpreted. There is little evidence that black slaves accepted their servitude because they believed God willed their slavery. The opposite is the case. The spirituals speak of God's liberation of black people, his will to set right the oppression of black slaves despite the overwhelming power of white masters. For blacks believed that there is an omnipotent, omnipresent, and omniscient power at work in the world, and that he is on the side of the oppressed and the downtrodden. As evidence they pointed to the blind man who received his sight, the lame who walked, and Lazarus who was received into God's kingdom while the rich man was rejected. And if "de God dat lived in Moses' time is jes' de same today", then God will vindicate the suffering of the righteous blacks and punish the unrighteous whites for their wrongdoings.' Starting from M. M. Fisher's fundamental analysis, Cone says: 'The divine liberation of the oppressed from slavery is the central theological concept in the black spirituals. These songs show that black slaves did not believe that human servitude was reconcilable with their African past and their knowledge of the Christian gospel. They did not believe that God created Africans to be the slaves of Europeans. Accordingly they sang of a God who was involved in history—*their* history—making right what whites have made wrong. . . . Because black people believed that they were God's children, they affirmed their somebodiness, refusing to reconcile their servitude with divine revelation.'

Some specialists believe that the Christians of Latin America and Africa will outnumber those of the other three continents in the year 2000. The majority of them, or at least a very considerable part, will belong to the spontaneous non-literary type of Pentecostal spirituality. It seems therefore that the spiritual and liturgical methods of the Black Pentecostal and Pentecostal-like communities in the USA will play a strategic role in the future, as they belong phenomenologically to the non-literary men, although they are living in the literary culture of America. That is why in future they may have to play an important role in the 'translation' from one culture into the other, both in the theological and the political realm.

Movements of social transformation

It becomes clear from the above that Black Pentecostalism and Black Power are not opposites, as some might wrongly suppose. A European observer might be inclined to consider black Pentecostalism as a religious mechanism of adaptation and Black Power as a political protest movement. This is not the case—at least not in this antithetic formulation. In a comparative study Luther P. Gerlach and Virginia Hine describe both as 'movements of social transformation'. By Pentecostalism they do not only mean black and white Pentecostals, but also the mushrooming and increasingly important charismatic groups within the main-line churches, particularly amongst Roman Catholic intellectuals. This destroyed the generally accepted theory that Pentecostal spirituality was bound to the milieu of the spiritually and materially poor. At their meetings one finds not the uneducated but the intellectuals, not the uncritical but the critical exegetes, not frustrated puritans but normal Christians. They do not only speak in tongues and pray, they eat together, they smoke and drink. Luther P. Gerlach has observed that people with a higher education are making the Pentecostal experience of baptism in the Spirit more readily than

25

students with an inferior education, or, he states, that speaking in tongues is less frequent amongst Pentecostal Mexicans than amongst white, middle-class Americans. The attempts to describe speaking in tongues as a pathological or half-pathological phenomenon of marginal people have been disproved by competent psychological and sociological studies in-so-far as it is possible to give objective criteria on that which has to be considered to be psychologically sound.

In their comparison between Black Power and Pentecostalism the two American anthropologists, who belong neither to Black Power nor to the Pentecostal movement, come to the conclusion that Black Power cannot be seen as a contrast to the Black Pentecostal movement. Both movements are religious and revolutionary and it is difficult to draw a dividing line between the two.

Pentecostalism is revolutionary because it offers alternatives to 'literary' theology and thus defrosts the 'frozen thinking' within literary forms of worship and committee-debate and gives the same chances to all—including the 'oral' people. It allows for a process of democratization of language by dismantling the privileges of abstract, rational and propositional systems, which—as is shown by the growth of the charismatic movement within the historical churches—is even experienced as beneficial by the intellectuals. Such examples of political alphabetization are not only found in the black Pentecostal churches in the USA, but also in the Russian, South African, Swedish and Latin American Pentecostal movements. Our socio-political search has entirely by-passed—and here the World Council of Churches must explicitly be mentioned amongst the culprits—this political and religious awakening, sometimes with a light undertone of regret for these religiously slightly doped believers.

Likewise Gerlach affirms that Black Power is a religious movement. He points to the conversion of Malcolm X to

26

Islam, which is responsible for the religious basis of the Black Muslim. Also in the rest of the Black Power movement their religious language is remarkable. They talk of 'transfiguration into blackness', the 'baptism into blackness' and see in Black Power *expressis verbis* a religion, into which one is initiated by an experience of commitment, a kind of conversion which is articulated in the framework of a liturgy.

It belongs furthermore to the essence of this cultural revolution that it develops fluid organizational forms, which our linear thinking can only understand with difficulty. It is led in a polycephalous way—i.e. by several heads—and finds its adherents through normal communication in everyday life, in the lower class particularly amongst relatives, in the upper class amongst the circle of friends. Their polycephalous executives change frequently. The different groups change their status in the whole framework of the movement from week to week. Only this polycephalous organization makes it possible for a minority to withstand a majority. The unity of the movement is not assured by normal headquarters but by 'travelling evangelists' (in the charismatic movement as well as in the Black Power movement) and through common code words and songs. It is easy, says Gerlach, to find out if a Black Power group is led by Communists. As soon as there are clear hierarchical structures, traceable executive centres, then we are dealing with a communist organization. And that is exactly why the very few communist-led Black Power groups are not revolutionary but reactionary, because they do not liberate black people from white tutelage, but replace one infantilising structure with another.

Likewise the transition from the charismatic movement to a Pentecostal church is recognizable by the emerging linear structure of dependence and direction. Such a transition from the polycephalous charismatic movement to a centrally organized church (be that along presbyterian, congregational or episcopal lines) can often be observed in the Pentecostal movement. But at the same time a new protest is kindled against the manipulative 'thinking from above', which either leads to the formation of a new charismatic revival (outside the organization in question) or calls back the organization to its initial polycephalous form.

In dealing with their attitude to opposition, Gerlach shows a further parallel. A kite flies against the wind. A revolutionary movement like Black Power or the Pentecostal Movement can only rise against the wind of opposition. That is why Black Power emerged in many towns only with the help of police action. In the same way many charismatic movements could only form themselves in the main-line churches with the help of the opposition of the ecclesiastical hierarchy to speaking in tongues.

Such a polycephalous revolutionary movement, says Gerlach, can only be counteracted effectively by 'overkill', i.e. by a rigorous control of all the media of communication, including the mail and the telephone, by arresting and eliminating all suspicious and sympathetic fellow-travellers, including those who are wrongly thought to be in sympathy with the movement. This method was used in earlier times in the Catholic church and in the national-socialistic state and is used at the present time in some parts of Russia. Yet in the United States—and one would like to add: in the Christian church—such a method is unthinkable. Therefore, Gerlach concludes, the ecclesiastical intervention against charismatic revolutionaries in the church and state intervention against Black Power are exactly that amount of wind which those movements need in order to rise and fly. It produces exactly the opposite of what is intended.

Tolerance and conviction

Gerlach's analysis is fascinating. But does it fit all situations? It seems to me that the revolutionary quality of such movements depends on two conditions which are logically exclusive of each other. Firstly they must have an almost axiomatic emotional and existential basis which cannot be shaken either through argument or through further investigation; or—if one prefers—they must rest on a religious conviction. But secondly they must allow question and criticism by fact and argument in order to prevent this religious conviction again becoming an ideological prison.

For the first thesis there are enough examples in the present day. Looked at objectively and rationally the Red Chinese were defeated by Chiang Kai Shek when they started their long march. Similarly the escalation of the bombardment of North Vietnam should have led to the capitulation of the North Vietnamese. However in both instances this was not the case. Why not? Gerlach answers that according to his conviction as an agnostic, religious commitment has such a power that it changes realities. One could also point to the success of the Pentecostals and Jesus People in dealing with drug addicts, where state institutions have almost completely failed. From this Gerlach draws a conclusion which is extremely relevant to the whole debate on development, namely that political and economic tinkering with the treatment of symptoms has to be replaced by the acknowledgment of these culturally revolutionary groups as catalysts of transformation.

For the second thesis Mao Tse Tung and the Pentecostal Movement provide again striking examples. The undifferentiated and unquestioned ideologies which prohibit tolerance and lay taboos on important questions by this very act destroy the original charismatic and revolutionary outbreak. What we then face is the well known keeping to the letter of the law—whether protestant, catholic or communist—by which people compensate for the sacrifices they have had to make by compelling others to make the same sacrifices. (Ersatz-Lust). Black Power and Pentecostalism have broken up institutionalized hypocrisy by taking literally that which was affirmed officially but not practised (in the church: the general priesthood of all believers; in the state: equal rights for black and white). Yet these movements become victims of institutionalized hypocrisy at the moment when they create a closed ideology of this revolutionary act. It seems that utter commitment and conviction does not allow for the 'luxury of tolerance'. Either a man is ready to risk everything for a recognizable goal, but then he is not prepared to be diverted from this goal by arguments or by facts; or he is a critical, liberal and tolerant man, but then he lacks that utter commitment which alone acts as a catalyst of transformation.

One may well ask: Can only fanatics be evangelists? Church history seems to answer this question in the affirmative. Neither the biblical prophets, nor the New Testament evangelists, nor the reformers, the theologians, evangelists and missionaries today, who are faithful to an utter commitment, are tolerant. The Pentecostals have sometimes said that the tolerance of many of today's Christians has its roots in their religious insecurity.

The Holy Spirit is a 'gentleman'

In spite of these obvious facts I am not prepared to accept a definite conflict between utter conviction and genuine tolerance. The Holy Spirit is a 'gentleman', the Pentecostals rightly say. If we have to use all our energies in order to press all critical arguments into our subconscious then we lack the necessary energy which we need for more differentiated tasks. To combine tolerance with utter conviction however demands the whole life and the whole energy of a man. In this sense lived tolerance can be understood as a concretization of the doctrine of justification by grace alone. If we really believe that we are sola gratia Christians, theologians, pastors, church bureaucrats, evangelists or politicians, then we will always have to reckon with the possibility that we might be wrong—and yet justified by God—and secondly that the one whom we want to convince will be justified by God sola gratia, even if he is wrong.

In relation to Black Power and to the Pentecostal Movement that would mean that we have to acknowledge equal rights to a non-literary theology. Only in the encounter between 'literary' and 'oral' cultures can we find out how far our 'literary' theology (i.e. our critical analytical methods) relates to pre- and post-rationality, and what the relationship is between 'the logic of the guts' and 'the logic of the brain'. Then we can ask: How does the dance speak to us and how does the word move us? How does the guitar talk and how does the thesis provide a variation on a theme? Or in an image: what is the reason that it is only the many colours of the rainbow in the spectrum of communication which can create that bright light which allows us to see reality? If God has given us a head, 'heart and reins' that we might know the world, he surely will not allow us to let one of these ways of perception wither. On the contrary we have to investigate how the head can learn from the heart-beat and the stomach from critical thinking.

These are not the questions of a specialist. In answering (or refusing to answer these questions) we decide whether the Church as a universal really catholic Church has a future, for the number of those Christians and theologians —if we are prepared to call them by this name—who look for and practise an oral theology as an alternative or complement to a rational and logical system of terms, is greatly increasing.

That is true for the growing African churches as well as for the Latin American churches, for the blacks of America and as of late for many young white people. The ecumenical problem of the immediate future is therefore not the relationship between catholic and protestant, but between 'oral' and 'literary' theology.

II. Flowers and Songs

A Mexican contribution to doing Theology

Is a theological dialogue possible between the Third World and the theological systems of Europe and America ? If there is any meaning in the ecumenical slogans 'Unity of Mankind, Unity of the Church' or 'Mission in Six Continents' then such a dialogue must be possible. But up to now the Third World has only made a theological appearance when it has made use of European-American concepts. Our theological partners from the Third World, who think differently from us either never make themselves heard or else lose interest in this theological debate. It becomes a luxury which they can only afford when it is subsidized from abroad. The rules of this theological game are ours even when the game is played in Nairobi or in Mexico. This is the main reason for the alarming fact that most of the Christian churches in the Third World are not members of the World Council and are largely disregarded in the fields of systematic theology, church history and missiology. Comb the theological literature of the past twenty years or the reports of the various committees of the World Council of Churches for theological contributions from the Third World and the result is lamentable. Philip Potter of the West Indies and

General Secretary of the World Council of Churches, gives the following explanation for this. It is easy, he says, to see why, for example, African delegates at the Fifth Assembly of the Lutheran World Federation in Evian in 1970 simply imitated traditional European theology :

> 'What opportunity had they to think about the faith in their own way? If they hadn't been "good boys" they would never have become church leaders. . . . We have seldom been allowed to think for ourselves. For long enough we have put up with a kind of theological imperialism. I call this racism. Unless we non-Westerners stick rigidly to the precise formulae of Western scholasticism, we are not considered theologians, or bright enough to communicate the Gospel.'

When the silenced again begin to speak

It is high time then, to look for non-Western categories for thinking theologically and presenting theology. The Division of World Mission and Evangelism of the World Council of Churches has been working on such experiments—and it means experiments ! The different road the World Council is seeking can only be found in dialogue with those people in the Third World who cannot and will not accept our modes of communication.

The historical background to such conversations in Mexico is interesting. The purpose of what the World Council of Churches is doing was described at a press conference in Mexico as the revolutionary movement 'which Christian faith not merely permits but positively requires' whereby 'men without a voice, men who have been reduced to silence by our intellectual concepts and racial prejudices should once again be allowed to speak and feel themselves to be equal partners. It means that the dialogue must not have a built-in advantage for the Westener. This is the revolution we seek. This, too, is what Paulo Freire is after. The rulers of Brazil fear this revolution more than they fear any **armed uprising. That** is why they jailed the former minister of education, Freire, for men who are aware of their dignity and significance are more dangerous than armed slaves'.

To make others develop a face

A thousand years ago Mexico had already developed one of the most advanced programmes of education and a fascinating philosophy. To formulate their philosophy, however, they did not create a system comparable with the system of an Aristotle, a Thomas Aquinas, or a Hegel. Miguel León-Portilla, the expert on ancient Mexican (Nahuatl) civilization, rightly points out that the quality of a philosophy, theology or theory of education cannot be judged by whether or not it creates a system. While there may be philosophers and theologians 'who still consider the construction of a coherent logical system to be the only form of philosophical thought' this is a mistaken attitude which if accepted would require us to exclude from discussion even such famous Western philosophers as Augustine, Pascal, Kierkegaard, Unamuno, Ortega and Bergson, not to mention Luther and the Bible.

The non-systematic philosophy of the ancient Mexicans did not prevent them from creating a compulsory educational programme which gave children in the humblest circumstances an equal opportunity of education with the nobility and royalty. The key figure in this education was the *tlamatini*, the wise man, 'he who knows things', 'he who knows something', 'the one who makes others develop a face, a personality'. 'He puts them, as it were, before a mirror and makes them discover themselves'. Under his influence people 'humanize their will'. The good *tlamatini*—like a good doctor—submits himself to practical criticism and even criticism of his methods and is ready to experiment. A bad *tlamatini*— like a bad doctor—keeps his tradition to himself. Like the lizard, he likes the dark corners; he deals in secret magic potions and in this way destroys men's faces, men's personality.

The educational medium was not the manual or the textbook but poetry. On this earth no one can declare the truth, said the *tlamatini*, except perhaps through 'flowers and songs'. If they wanted to be precise they did not call for sharper definitions but described what they meant by referring to two of its most remarkable features (*difrasismo*). For example, they described a woman as 'skirt and blouse', a city as 'water and hill' and the transcendence of God as 'night and wind'. Like a hunter, the *tlamatini* was chasing songs, he 'steals flowers and songs', 'butterflies of song'.

This approach refused to express the inexpressible. Hence the scepticism and agnosticism of the Nahuas. Can we say anything certain about the future, about life after death, or even about life's meaning? This scepticism finds final expression in the question : Does man possess any truth ? What was in question here was not man's sincerity. It was the much more radical question as to whether man could possess truth at all. Both the nature of truth and the world of goods we have to 'consider as lent to us, oh friends'.

Enter the 'true faith' !

With the arrival of the Spaniards, the songs died away, the flowers were trampled under foot, the quetzal-feathers torn out. The philosophy of the Mexicans was despised as superstition, even though on the basis of their educational programme of 'flowers and songs' the Mexicans had developed a mathematics, an astronomy and an architecture which still moves us to admiration today. The books of the Nahuatl people were burned, their temples plundered, their language suppressed, their teachers and priests put to death. Las Casas, a catholic missionary and

36

defender of the Indians estimated that 12 million Indians died in 38 years, mostly as slaves in the mines.

The last testimony of the Nahuas is found in the contemporary record of the discussion which some of the *tlamatinime* had with the newly arrived Spanish missionaries. The missionaries urged them earnestly to abhor, to despise, to curse and spit on the gods they had worshipped. The Mexicans answered courteously that they were fully aware of the difficulties and dangers the Spaniards had had to endure in crossing the ocean :

> 'Our Lords, our very esteemed Lords: great hardships have you endured to reach this land . . .'
> 'You said
> that we know not
> the Lord of the Close Vicinity,
> to Whom the heavens and the earth belong.
> You said
> that our gods are not true gods.
> New words are these
> that you speak;
> because of them we are disturbed,
> because of them we are troubled.'

But how could the missionaries say such offensive things ? The Mexicans had known God for centuries, in-so-far as He can be known by anyone. What the missionaries wanted them to believe they did not believe to be true, even if to say this offended the missionaries. Then, simply and impressively, the Mexicans confessed :

> 'Allow us then to die,
> let us perish now,
> since our gods are already dead.'

A heretic defends the Indians

From about 1509 Catholic legal experts held it to be necessary, before embarking on war, to justify this step to the heathen peoples of Latin America and to call upon these peoples to surrender voluntarily. 'This official proclamation (known as the *requerimiento*) was obligatory from the year 1513 ... The country's inhabitants were informed that there was only one God and that His representative was the Pope in Rome and furthermore that the latter had given their territories to the kings of Spain. The people were then required to accept and submit to the Christian faith. Wilful refusal to do so would bring on them war, all kinds of misfortune, the enslavement of them all together with their wives and children, since they would be rebels against their rightful lord. Since no one, of course, submitted voluntarily, the slaughter began.' Those who did submit were nevertheless enslaved. One of the few to challenge these practices was the Dominican, Fray Bartolomé de las Casas. Briefly and sharply he branded as unjust all the wars fought by the Spaniards. 'The supposedly glorious feats of Spanish heroes are gross iniquities. Spain will still have to pay for this to the last farthing. She has failed in the task entrusted to her and proved herself unfit to derive the least material benefit from these colonial lands.' Accordingly Fray Bartolomé refused absolution to the departing soldiers. The Emperor Charles V should restore all the property he had unjustly seized. We are not surprised to learn that people reviled Las Casas as a heretic, antichrist and a Lutheran.

The controversy came to a head in the disputation between Las Casas and Juan Ginés de Sepúlveda in 1550-1557. Sepúlveda gave four reasons to justify war against the heathen :

1. The heinous character of their sins, particularly their idolatry and sins against nature.
2. Because of their primitive condition, they had a duty to serve the more advanced Spaniards and if they refused could be compelled by war to do so.
3. For the sake of the preaching of the Gospel for which the way could only be prepared by conquest.

4. To free the innocent human beings destined for sacrifice and, in some cases, to wipe out cannabalism.

Las Casas' reply to the first point was that the sins of the heathen did not come within the competence of the church. 'For what have I to do with judging outsiders? . . . God judges those outside', said St. Paul (I Cor. 5. 12f.). To the second point he replied by denying that the Indians were merely uncouth barbarians. He answered the third point by contrasting Christ who sent His apostles forth as sheep among wolves and who told his disciples that they must be ready to lay down their lives for His sake. War brought in its train enormities, hatred, fear and falsehood. As for protecting the innocent the evils of war far outweighed any possible benefits.

Ruins

Las Casas was not heeded. All that is left, therefore, of the Mexican educational system, the Mexican language, art and architecture is—ruins. It is not unfair to say that Mexico's present widespread illiteracy and economic dependence were created by Europeans and maintained by Americans. The invasion and conquest of Mexico was the beginning of a long martyrdom. It is still going on before our very eyes. The *mestizos* and the Indians, 'out of a sense of the profoundest spiritual shame, hardly dare to raise their heads. The problem of the peasant is not simply that he has only a few coins in his purse. It is something more, which reduces him to something less than a man', says Oscar Maldonado, a Mexican Roman Catholic priest.

Yet in a fragmentary way the ancient Mexican tradition lives on. Even the remains of the sculptures, temples and books compel the admiration of the visitor to the Anthro-

39

pological Museum in Mexico. But the ruins that are left are not only those of stone. There are remnants of the Mexican tradition which are discovered, for example, when priests and nuns join with the *campesinos* in excavating the buried humanity of the ancient Mexicans. The peasants can once again recover 'their face'. But we also meet this ancient Mexican tradition in the Mexican Pentecostal movement (which is at least 50% of Mexican Protestantism). These Pentecostals develop their own social and economic life—perhaps even their own theology—independently of the American missionaries. One of these churches is the *Iglesia Cristiana Independiente Pentecostés* with 150,000 members. Her founder was Andrés Ornelas Martínez (died 1958), a miner from San Juan de Los Lagos in the Mexican state of Jalisco. Shortly after the First World War he emigrated to Miami (Arizona) where somebody gave him a Spanish edition of the Book of Proverbs. The book at first sight did not interest him. On his return to his native village he began reading it because he was bored, and he found it interesting. But the last pages in the book were missing, so he ordered the whole 'Book of Proverbs' from the address in Los Angeles printed at the bottom of the title page. He received some tracts, the whole Book of Proverbs and a New Testament. The study of the New Testament captivated him so much that when others were sleeping at night he went into the countryside in order to pray, to confess his sins and to ask God that he might use him for something worthwhile. In December 1920 he travelled again to Miami in search of a complete Bible. Overhearing a fellow-miner uttering the word 'Bible' he asked him: 'Do you have a Bible? Can you show it to me?' He could hardly wait for the end of the shift in order to see the Bible. The colleague took him to his pastor who gave Andrés Ornelas a Bible. (This Bible is kept today at the headquarters of the Iglesia Cristiana Independiente Pentecostés, Pachuco.)

In May 1921 he returned to Mexico and went first to the services of the Methodists in Pachuco (Hgo). There he met Raymundo Nieto, who introduced him into the Pentecostal baptism of the Spirit and baptized him in October 1922 in a river. But already in June 1922 the two had founded a Pentecostal congregation in Pachuco which is considered today as the mother-church of the Iglesia Cristiana Independiente Pentecostés. By their fearless testimony, the healing of the sick and their practical Christianity they won a number of followers. However, that was also the time when the government favoured protestantism because of its antipathy to the Catholic Church. In 1927 Raymundo was not any longer 'considered to be in a position to continue his pastorate' (as Ramírez puts it). Ornelas became the pastor of the Pachuco church.

By amalgamation with other different churches, amongst them one which had been founded by the Swedish Pentecostal missionary Axel Anderson (Filadelfia Church, and renamed Saron Church) in Mexico City, the organization grew steadily. In 1941 Ornelas disassociated himself from the foreign missionaries. In 1953 he was successful in pulling together two hundred congregations into one organization. 'It was an historic act when he threw away the yoke of the bad foreigners and their Mexican paladines', states the official journal of the church in a short historical account. In 1955 the church amalgamated with the important Iglesia Evangélica Independiente. The united church is called today—after further amalgamations —Iglesia Cristiana Independiente Pentecostés. Very early they sent their missionaries to Colombia and Puerto Rico. A bank, El Banco del Fondo Común, was founded. Ramírez proudly relates in the preface to his history of

41

the church: 'The movement is genuinely indigenous. It does not receive subsidies from any foreign country or mission.'

Ixmiquilpan

'The Mesquital region of the state of Hidalgo in Mexico is one of the driest and poorest places of the country. Prairie-like valleys are framed by yellow mountains. During the day the sun burns mercilessly and at night it can become very cold, as the valleys are 6,000 feet above sea-level.' (Tschuy).

Industrialization which invaded Mexico City, Monterrey and Guadalajara in the fifties, has not yet reached the region of Mesquital, where agriculture and a small cottage industry give a very meagre income and where in 1960 more than half of the population still spoke the Indian Otomí language. Those Indians can again be divided into half who speak Otomí exclusively and those who, beside their Indian language, have mastered some Spanish. More than a third are illiterate.

The results of the political and social revolution, which conquered the big cities between 1910 and 1917, reached the country of the Otomí much later. Far into the thirties one could find hardly any Protestants here. Those who dared to confess the new faith were either driven away or killed.

That is why in 1936 a young Indian, by the name of Venancio Hernandez had to leave his native valley and the hacienda where he and his ancestors had worked since the arrival of the Spaniards. After having taught himself to read and write, he managed somehow to get hold of a Bible. He began to read it, at first very sceptically because he knew that the great Mexican revolution was very consciously anti-ecclesiastical if not anti-religious. As an Indian he knew too how the religion of

42

the conquerors had been thrust on the native population often by brute force and how the hierarchy of the church sided at the time of the war of independence at the beginning of the 19th century with the Spaniards and the foreign king.

Yet the Bible which Venancio Hernandez now read appeared to him to be entirely different. The Christ which it described was not half hidden by the Virgin Mary or the Saints. He was neither a poor and feeble child nor a thorn-crowned, weeping, dying or even dead son of God. On the contrary: he spoke with authority, he showed courage, he did not fear the mighty ones of this world nor the indignation of the people who had expected another Messiah. Such a personality would have fitted the Mexican revolution well! More: this Christ talked with individual people about their sin, their *lostness,* about the revelation of God through this Christ, on his love for man, on his sacrificial death, by which he reconciled man with God. One only had to accept this gift . . . ! Why had somebody never brought such a message to Venancio Hernandez? The Virgin Mary, the Saints, the places of pilgrimage and the indulgences: all this was not at all necessary if that book were true. And it was true, for he acquired an inner confidence which had been unknown to him hitherto. Here was a message which finally gave the right spiritual guidance to his revolutionary thinking and his search for social and political justice.

Venancio Hernandez did not want to and could not remain silent. During the siesta he read to the other farm workers from the wonderful book. They believed and were converted, changed their old habits and all of a sudden, under a tree, where they assembled, the listeners were transformed into a small congregation.

The owner of the hacienda was informed that some of his Indian farm workers had become Protestants. He summoned Venancio Hernandez and his friends before him and prohibited them to have any further religious meetings. The Indians did not answer. But common prayer and Bible reading went on. The owner of the hacienda, the local priest and other Indians agreed on driving out the small congregation from their valley under threat of death.

Under the leadership of Venancio they wandered across into the next valley to the village of Ixmiquilpan where the main road from Mexico City to Guadalajara passes. Outside the village, on a little hill on which the army had installed a small observation post, the small group settled down taking advantage of the military post which gave them a certain protection. Hernandez knew that the small congregation had to stick together if it were not to risk its sudden death. It was at this time that the system of land reform limited estate ownership to at the most five hundred hectares. That is why one of the big land owners of Ixmiquilpan had to sell part of his land. Venancio and his followers approached him and managed to get a favourable contract. They bought a good piece of land with irrigation rights. As they possessed very little cash, the former owner allowed them to repay the amount of the purchase price by instalments. The small evangelical community of Christians had impressed him and, in spite of pressure from other quarters, he gave them a chance. 'God has been with us!' said Venancio ponderingly when recalling those pioneer days.

A Pentecostal co-operative

The newly acquired farm land was under collective ownership, but the land on which the small stone houses were now gradually being built and the family gardens were privately owned—up to this time the Indians had lived only in Cactus huts. They organized themselves in agricultural co-operatives and built a co-operative textile factory which they continue to modernize. Compared with technical advances in Europe and America their tools and machines are modest. Yet the outstanding fact is that the Indians have created it themselves. Therefore they are not dependent on foreign finance and expertise— even in the form of missionaries—for this handicraft production fits in with their tradition. However it has to be admitted that these Indians are unusually gifted both intellectually and manually. With precision and expertise such an Indian will install a projector together with a generator (in order to produce the necessary electricity) and will not forget to check all the contacts carefully. He is also able to service and repair his versatile agricultural tractor himself.

Their church had to undergo heavy persecutions years ago from the local Catholic clergy. 'Sometimes the priest said that we were not good people, even that we were of the devil', they recalled later to Maria Amerlinck who made a careful anthropological study of the Pentecostal church at Ixmiquilpan. 'In fact', Maria Amerlinck comments, 'persecution had not been initiated by the priests, but by some of the richer people of Ixmiquilpan who could count on the local political structure and who disliked the acquiring of land by the Indians. Yet with the help of regional and national political forces and with some economic help from outside the difficulties were overcome.' Pentecostals considered it to be their duty not to respond to persecution with vengeance. 'By praying and reading the Bible they searched for the will of God and instead of exercising vengeance they offered pardon. The murderers recognized their wickedness, repented and became members of the church.' (Tschuy).

When the governor of their state needed workers for

building roads, they made the following offer: 'We know', they said, 'that you want to build roads in our region but that you lack workers. We will provide three hundred men daily free of charge if you provide machines and technical know-how. That is how we are going to show to you that we "cristianos" are useful citizens.' By this demonstration they were able to prove better than by a theoretical statement that they were not—as their persecutors affirmed—sectarian, but responsible members of society. During the road-building they composed new songs in the soft restrained style of the Otomí. Today these songs form part of their liturgy and remind them of the time of persecution and how it was overcome.

Dangers from outside

The church is no longer threatened by the Catholics. Indeed the latter are ready to learn from Venancio who has, for example, been made a member of the Advisory Theological Commission of the Catholic Church of Mexico. Today the church is threatened by a different 'true faith'. I was personally present at a service in Ixmiquilpan at which an American missionary was the preacher. At the beginning of the service three young Indians came forward with their guitars, knelt down and quietly prayed. Then they played and sang with a cultured restraint and manner which was extremely moving. Even the members of the congregation did not sing at the top of their voices, as one usually finds in Pentecostal circles. But then came the missionary's sermon! His words went back and forth across the Indian congregation like a steamroller. The Indians gently lowered their heads but even so I thought it scarcely possible for them to sustain this flood of oratory without injury. But four centuries have developed in them a capacity to remain dignified and noble even in humiliation. When the appeal for conversion was issued, many of them came to the front, covered their face with their *rebozos* and quietly wept. Before the end of the service the missionary and his entourage quit the chapel. In the house of the chief a large table was spread with a dozen varied Mexican dishes, lovingly and skilfully prepared, together with native fruits and drinks. The missionary talked incessantly—in English, which the Otomí do not understand—while the chief stood at the door with his wife and served the guests. When the food had disappeared, everyone rose. 'Excuse me,' said the Indian chief, 'I have a sick friend and I would like you to pray for him.' 'Of course', answered the missionary. 'Let us pray.' And in his booming voice he rattled off a prayer: 'Lord, You can heal even from afar. Make our unfortunate friend well. Amen. But now we have to be going.' And with that, he went. But Venancio was sorry for him. How could the missionary be blamed for being a *gringo*!

Conversion and Development

The secret of Venancio's congregation lies in its theological and economic independence. I cannot find out exactly when Venancio united his congregation with the Iglesia Cristiana Independiente Pentecostés whose headquarters are in the nearby Pachuco. He is head pastor and has under him about forty *obreros*, lay preachers who in addition to their work as farmers and craftsmen serve about forty congregations each numbering about a hundred.

The upward social movement of the members of the church is phenomenal. 'There is a close link between evangelism and the search for education', says Maria Amerlinck, a Catholic anthropologist. Giving their testimony, participating in the life of the congregation, financing the church themselves, 'develops' the gifts which

47

are latent in these Indians to their full potential. For them 'giving' (money, animals, vegetables, even drinks) to the church is not 'alms-giving', because God is not a beggar (*limosnero*). She sums up her assessment as follows: 'Under these circumstances religious conversion is the only way out of the narrow confines of traditionalism . . . The Indians need this new ideology as a means of rationalization which enables them to understand their relationship to the changing world around them and gives a definite dignity to the individual person.'

While in the Catholic church in Ixmiquilpan most of the priests are foreigners, the Pentecostals have exclusively native ministers (who almost without exception earn their living in secular work). Before their conversion most of them were employed as farm workers on a day-to-day basis. Today most of them are farm-owners, masons, owners of small shops and mills, lorry drivers and mechanics.

The Pentecostal pastors do not consider their ministry as a purely religious ministry which would distinguish and separate them from the rest of the population. They do not see themselves as paid specialists of religion, but very much more as 'economic evangelists' of a kind, or 'evangelistic development advisers'. They earn their own living because their example and the way in which they build their own houses (many of them are masons!) is part of their proclamation. They feel themselves to be superior to the Catholic priests and are very proud of their special ministry of evangelism. They criticize the priests openly—and, if opportunity arises, also the Catholic hierarchy—because they work solely as priests and lay themselves open to the reproach that they exercise their ministry for money. Discussing the question of a full-time and paid ministry, they said: 'What would our colleagues at work say? As a full-time ministry we would become estranged from them.' Hernandez resumes the theology of their *lived fellowship* in these words: 'The community believes in the salvation of the hands by work, of the mind by learning to read, of the body by divine healing and of the soul by new birth.' (Tschuy)

There is no doubt that the Otomí have created an example of development policy which by its very simplicity is fascinating. In this they have explicitly included the women—a revolutionary act in their society. Here and there, but very reluctantly, there are the beginnings of a dialogue with European theology and churches (Niemoeller). The attempt is not without dangers. Maria Amerlinck draws attention to the growing paternalism, particularly by the leaders in Pachuco. Their theological and economic independence is impressive and was a matter of life and death in the pioneering phase of the church. But will it last in the more complex economic situation of the future? And what will the Otomí do if they are restricted by political and economic power structures which cannot be overcome easily by their methods of self-help?

It is also possible that in a wider sphere the intelligence, the charm and the theological understanding of the Indians will produce a solution which we Europeans have not discovered yet. But in order to give any solution the necessary scope, their buried humanity and culture must be excavated in a broader, in an ecumenical, field. I was involved in the attempt of such an ecumenical excavation expedition.

Excavating the ruins

In order to avoid even more destruction by our excavation, we had to find someone in Mexico who could talk both with intellectuals and with people with little or no formal education, since our 'excavation' was not to be restricted to the Indians but to cover all sections of the Mexican people and be a joint discovery made with their participation. We worked on the assumption that it was both possible and desirable to initiate a theological dialogue between intellectuals and illiterate people, Mexican Indians, European Mexicans and half-breeds, Jesuit college lecturers and Adventist roadworkers, journalists and Pentecostal preachers, Methodists of the middle class, and Indian Mormons. The invitation to the 'discussions' had to be conveyed personally so as not to prejudice the illiterate. Miss Maria Antonieta Hernández, a lecturer in Christian Education in the Comunidad Teológica of Mexico was the right person for this job. Her unmistakable Mexican appearance overcame any mistrust on the part of the Indians and *campesinos*, Pentecostals and Mormons. As an Anglican she had access to both Protestants and Catholics. Through her flair for the 'flowers and songs' mode of communication she aroused the curiosity of journalists and television people. What were the results of the excavation? Since detailed reports of the six seminars held in the spring of 1970 in Monterrey, Mexico, Merida, Amecameca and Guadalajara have been published in Spanish, I confine myself to summarizing some of the main points that were discussed.

The 'flowers and songs' method

A theological discussion on the basis of fictional or biblical stories, making use of films and pictures, seemed to most participants the obvious approach. The showing of the film 'Parable'—a silent film depicting the passion and resurrection of Christ using the medium of a clown's martyrdom—provoked objections from some Methodist and Baptist intellectuals. Christ could not be presented in the symbol of a clown, they believed. 'Why not?' demanded a coloured worker (a Pentecostal preacher). 'This film shows the circus of life in which we are all performers whether we like it or not. We dance just like puppets, to the pattern decided by those who manipulate the strings. *Gracias a Dios,* Christ came, put himself in our place that we might be set free, that we might be men with a face.'

In the discussion of the four different versions of the story of Peter's Confession (Mk. 8, 27-33; Mt. 16, 13-23; Lk. 9, 18-22; Jn. 6, 66-71), two groups came to the following conclusion: 'It is hardly possible to formulate a modern confession of faith in conceptual terms. Confessing the faith today presupposes an on-going exchange, mutual correction and relation to constantly changing situations. We can, however, see four elements which must be there in any confession of faith:

★ 'A confession of faith today requires various confessions. This variety can sometimes even include mutually contradictory confessions. We could not agree whether this pluralism had to be confined to various biblical positions or could be extended to include new positions not represented in the Bible.

★ 'Confessing the faith (*martyria*) involves the element of suffering.

★ 'Every confession of faith must be related to the history of Jesus of Nazareth.

★ 'The test as to whether a confession of faith is biblical or merely a human invention is ecumenical discussion crossing racial, confessional, social, national and sexual boundaries.'

The human and the holy

The story of the 'Guardian Angel' by Gerardo Murillo tells of a rather uncouth but kind-hearted woman who takes in her care a young girl whose mother

51

has been wrongly imprisoned for some months. By her courage and persistence she secures the mother's release. The discussion started from the question: In what sense was this woman a 'guardian angel'? In answering this question some took the traditional line and separated the action of the Holy Spirit (or of the angel) from purely human sympathy, while others maintained that the woman, being of divine origin as a human person, was in fact an instrument of the Holy Spirit in spite of her crude language and her penchant for alcohol.

This finding made necessary further discussion of the relationship between the Lukan and Pauline pneumatologies in the New Testament. During this fascinating discussion one of the *campesinos* formulated the following pneumatology: 'Training in the Bible and the liturgy is not a condition for the work of the Holy Spirit in a human being. The Holy Spirit has been given to the whole of mankind.' To the objection that the Holy Spirit only works in those who are obedient to Him, one *campesina* said this: 'That's not true. Mary Magdalene, for example, who approached Jesus with a desire to win him, put on a very revealing robe and covered Jesus with a very seductive perfume. Of course she wasn't ready to receive the gift of Jesus. But Jesus looked on her and gave all he had to give.' Astonishingly, it was a Catholic who put forward this evangelical interpretation.

Non-Christian religions

In connection with the story of the Ethiopian eunuch (Acts 8, 26-40), the question was raised whether baptism was essential to salvation. The information that the critical verse 37 is absent from certain manuscripts stirred up no fundamentalist feelings as sometimes happens in Europe. In general, when the two-source theory was mentioned (only as an hypothesis) and during detailed discussion of form-criticism of Peter's confession, no one asked the anguished question which inevitably arises in Europe: 'What is there left to believe?' The facts were noted but the question which mattered more for these people was: What is the relevance of these facts?

In discussing the story of the Ethiopian eunuch, a Jesuit explained that Philip's interpretation of the Isaiah passage (Is. 53, 7-8) in Acts 8, 32-33 conflicts with that of the exegetes of his day. The question therefore arises as to the authority of Philip's exegesis, interpreting the Isaiah passage as referring to Jesus. Are there not events and texts which have today to be interpreted in terms of Jesus, in opposition to both Christian and non-Christian tradition? 'There are disciples of Jesus Christ outside the Church. The external sign of being a Christian is not therefore baptism, nor abstinence from alcohol and nicotine, nor the pictures of saints in our homes, but the discovery that Jesus Christ is greater than our theological and political ideas, indeed, greater than our faith.'

Some Indian Mormons 'excavated' the buried concerns of their forefathers within the traditional Mormon fiction-history, with its insistence on the appearance of Christ on the American continent before the arrival of Columbus. What they were primarily concerned with was not the historical accuracy of this statement but its function, namely the expression of the faith that even the ancient Mexicans had received a revelation from God. They also wanted to know, therefore, whether the Christian revelation had been made once and for all or whether there was still revelation today. When this was affirmed—with the qualification that present-day revelation must be considered in relation to its source and be corrected in ecumenical discussion—the decisive question was put: Is this process of correction a mutual one? What they were obviously concerned to do was to excavate the buried testimonies of their past and to see them afresh in the light of the revelation of Christ. God's ways here too are strange: this illuminating suggestion came from Mormon Indians, of all people!

A Protestant reader may well ask: where in all this is the centre of the Gospel, justification by faith? It was already formulated above in the story of Mary Magdalene, in the insight that being a Christian transcends the traditional expressions of Christian faith. Perhaps it is also there in the view of one group about the theology of the Yahwist, which concluded with the wish—'We need today prophets like the Yahwist to make it clear to the Church that it lives solely by God's mercy and not on the basis of its faith and Christian achievements.'

Mexico is usually regarded as a secularized country. Theological and religious topics are seldom taken up by the mass media. It was all the more surprising therefore to find the Monterrey television devoting an hour's programme to that kind of interpretation of the Bible and the press reporting it as an 'active, practical school of Christian renewal'. This dialogue was described as a 'faithful exegesis of Holy Scripture' unlike the methods of indoctrination and polemics.

III. Pentecost of N'Kamba

The Catholicity of The Kimbanguist Church

Neither in the strictly dogmatical nor in the historical sense does the *Eglise de Jésus-Christ sur la terre d'après le prophète Simon Kimbangu* (EJCSK) belong to the Pentecostal movement. Their practice of Spirit baptism, for example, is unknown amongst Pentecostals. In contrast to other independent churches in Africa, the Kimbanguist Church did not emerge from Pentecostal missionary work. But on the other hand there are remarkable parallels between Pentecostals and Kimbanguists: healing through prayer; spontaneous worship within the framework of unwritten, but nevertheless efficient, liturgies; the congregation as a brotherly, all-embracing community; the hierarchical leadership of the church; speaking in tongues, trembling and visions. Above all both Kimbanguists and Pentecostals believe that the Holy Spirit can be experienced and that evil spirits are best counteracted by the power of the Spirit. When at the Central Committee of the World Council of Churches in Canterbury (1969) the Brazilian Pentecostal church *Brasil para Cristo* was admitted to the World Council together with the Kimbanguist Church, the Brazilian Pentecostal leader Manoel de Melo named the *chef spirituel* of the Kimban-

55

guists, Joseph Diangienda, a Pentecostal, while the latter promoted de Melo to be a Kimbanguist.

Pentecostal Movement and Kimbanguists in Zaïre

The British and North American Assemblies of God, the Norwegian and two different groups of Swedish Pentecostals, as well as the British Congo Evangelistic Mission and the French Assemblées de Dieu, work in Zaïre. The history of these Pentecostal missions—including the remarkable school and hospital work of the Norwegian and Swedish Pentecostals—is described in detail in the French edition of my *'The Pentecostals'*.

It seems that the different Pentecostal missions hardly have any contact with each other, possibly because the different missions work in different parts of this large country. In this the Pentecostal missions in Zaïre are fundamentally different from those in South Africa, as there one finds a certain co-operation between the different Pentecostal churches. Furthermore the Pentecostal movement in Zaïre has not produced a leader of the quality of Nicholas Bhengu, who is successful in blending Pentecostal spirituality with an elementary political alphabetization.

Marie-Louise Martin mentions 46 Protestant missionary societies and churches in Zaïre—many of them evangelical. The protest of the youth against 'the treacherous and merchandising missionaries' is therefore understandable:

'In considering today the necessity of decolonizing mentally the brain of certain Congolese who have been pushed by the European and American Christians to boycott the work of the Eglise de Christ au Congo, in using existing divisions which have been imported from the West by missionaries who are already divided in their home-country . . . , and taking into account that conscientious Congolese should not follow the pride of the foreign (white) Christians who have torn asunder the body of Christ, the Second National Congress of the Protestant Youth Union in the Congo . . . expresses its indignation before the separatist attitude of the Congolese Christians being in the foreign (missionary) Christians' pay thus making themselves part of the power of high finance in order to perpetuate on Congolese ground a reactionary evangelical Spirit which has been overcome by the ideals of the Congolese revolution.'

One would have hoped that there would be co-operation at least between Pentecostals and Kimbanguists in Zaïre, and one can see a few encouraging signs here. While it is true the rejection of the black Pentecostal churches in South Africa finds its parallel in the rejection of the Kimbanguists by the American Assemblies of God, at present—and this is a new development—the voices of those Pentecostals, who see in the Kimbanguists their brothers, are increasing. The German Pentecostal Christian Krust reports the Fourth Assembly of the World Council of Churches at Uppsala in 1968 as follows:

'Hitherto I had known nothing of the existence of such a church [namely the Kimbanguist church]. But when, after greeting and introducing ourselves, we knelt down and prayed together, the two [Kimbanguist] brethren from the Congo joined in prayer. It is true that I understand French only partially and it was not possible for me to follow the exact wording of their prayer but the way in which they prayed and spoke with God, that made a tremendous impression on me and the others in the prayer-room: These brothers are specially inspired by the Holy Spirit! They spoke with such dignity and serenity that it warmed one's heart. In the subsequent informal discussion the impression was deepened that those two brothers [Jean-Claude L. Luntatila, Philip Nanga] were firmly rooted in faith, that they were true members of the body of Christ, born again and baptized with the Holy Spirit.'

One can only hope that the Assemblies of God will change their unfavourable judgment of the Kimbanguists ('a false Christ religion') in the light of the reports of European Pentecostals.

My assessment is based on confidential documents and correspondence in the archives of the World Council of Churches; on personal interviews with Kimbanguists in Geneva; on the specialized literature mentioned in the bibliography; on the analysis by the Swiss theologian Marie-Louise Martin, and on the unpublished research of Werner Ustorf of Hamburg.

Marie-Louise Martin had access to documents relevant to the origin of the church and was able to interview eye-witnesses. That enabled her to recognize many stories and reports as legends and to discard them. Some of these legends appeared in 1961 in a small liturgy, allegedly published by Kimbanguist pastors with the approval of their spiritual head. Though this booklet has often been used as source-material by researchers it is doubtless a forgery, among other reasons because the Kimbanguists did not use printed liturgies.

Werner Ustorf, however, has serious doubts whether Marie-Louise Martin's description presents anything more than the stream-lined 'orthodox' view of Kimbanguism as it is presented today by its urban leadership. He attempted a thorough reconstruction of the life and death of Simon Kimbangu on the basis of hitherto unknown or forgotten documents (among them two letters by Simon Kimbangu). A more detailed discussion of his approach, which will surely be highly controversial, must wait until he has published his research.

Simon Kimbangu

The Kimbanguist church goes back to Simon Kimbangu, born in 1889 at N'Kamba Thysville (Lower Zaïre). Kuyela his father and his mother Lwezi died early. He was educated by his aunt, Kinzembo. As a young man he became a Christian. He had his theological education from the Baptists and in July 1915 he was baptized in the river that passes by at Ngombe-Lutete together with his wife Mvilu Marie and Mikala Mandombe who later became his assistant. He was a farmer by profession and occasionally helped his cousin who was a carpenter.

One night in the year 1918 when many died of flu because the medical help promised by the missions did not arrive, Kimbangu heard a voice saying: 'I am Christ, my servants are unfaithful, I have chosen you to witness and convert your brothers . . . Take care of my sheep'. Simon answered: 'I do not know this kind of work, Lord. There are others better educated than me, they will take care of the flock'. Night after night the audition was repeated and Simon's wife heard Simon answering.

On the morning of the 6th of April, 1921 (today celebrated as the foundation-day of the church)—Simon went to the market. Against his will he felt compelled to go into the neighbouring village of Ngombe-Kinsukke, to enter the hut of Nkiantondo, a sick woman, to lay his hands on her head and to heal her in the name of Christ. The woman was healed. Soon other healings followed. Marie-Louise Martin sums up this period: 'The most important point made by Kimbanguist narrators is: "Should the same not happen in the Congo as happened in Palestine? Has the time of miracles passed? Did Christ not ordain his disciples to preach *and* to heal? If we recall the stories in the Acts of the Apostles, did they not do it in the power of the Holy Ghost?" '

'According to the Kimbanguists a new Pentecost had arrived. The Holy Ghost had obviously come to Simon Kimbangu and equipped him with power to heal.' This conviction is so great that the trinitarian formula 'in the name of the father, the son and the Holy Ghost' is often supplemented by the words 'which has come upon

Simon Kimbangu' or 'which has spoken to us through Simon Kimbangu'. 'That does not mean, as has been stated, that Simon Kimbangu replaces the Holy Spirit in the eyes of his followers, but it does mean that they consider him to be an instrument of the Holy Spirit.'

Now the masses flocked together. Without wanting it, Kimbangu became the founder of a large and enthusiastic movement which shook the whole country. With the Bible in his hands he asked his countrymen to destroy all witchcraft, to abstain from heathen dances and from polygamy. Surprised by great success he chose five African helpers. But the missionaries and the then Belgian colonial government became very suspicious. He was unjustly accused of hatred of the European, of seducing people into refusing to pay their taxes and into laziness.

In the name of law and order . . .

The Belgian civil servant Morel was asked to open an investigation of the Kimbanguist revival. When Morel arrived at N'Kamba the prophet and his five disciples felt the Spirit upon them and they spoke in tongues and sang throughout the whole night.

Morel came to the conclusion: 'Kimbangu wants to found a religion which reflects the mentality of the Africans, a religion, which contains the fundamentals of protestantism, mixed up with practices of witchcraft . . . Everybody can see that the European religions have been petrified by abstractions and do not correspond to the mentality of the Africans who are longing for tangible facts and protection from demons. The religion of Kimbangu suits them because it is supported by tangible facts.' And Marie-Louise Martin adds: 'How right Morel was. But the time to evaluate this insight positively had not yet come!' for Morel continues: 'Therefore it is necessary to fight Kimbangu. His tendency is pan-African.

Natives will say: "We have found a God of the blacks, a religion which corresponds to the Africans" . . . Law and Order demands that Kimbanguism be stopped quietly but immediately.'

When the colonial government decided to arrest Kimbangu, he fled from N'Kamba but in September 1921 of his own free will he presented himself before his persecutors. Before that he admonished his followers to accept sufferings courageously, never to use the sword and never to repay the evil done by the Europeans by doing evil to them. Although no white man was ever injured, Kimbangu was arrested in September 1921 after only five months of public ministry. In a pseudo-process the Belgian writer Chome called it a 'juridicial monstrosity'—the military commander Rossi sentenced him to 120 lashes, followed by capital punishment. However, the Belgian King, Albert I, commuted capital punishment to life imprisonment, partly because of intercessions by some missionaries. Kimbangu was deported to Katanga where he was imprisoned for thirty years. He died in the prison of Elisabethville (today Lubumbashi) on the 12th October 1951. J. van Wing (whose report was also obviously used by the Assemblies of God) stated that on his death-bed Kimbangu had agreed to become a Catholic, but this statement is categorically denied by the Sisters who had looked after Kimbangu in prison and by one of his warders.

Sufferings

Kimbangu accepted his imprisonment without putting up any resistance. Likewise he admonished his followers not to exercise any opposition. He left nothing to his disciples but the Bible and the advice to join the Protestant missions. In spite of this the Kimbanguists were now faced with a cruel persecution which lasted almost forty years. About 37,000 heads of families were deported (this means about 100,000 persons) and most of them died in exile. It was sufficient to be accused of being a Kimbanguist or to utter the name of Simon Kimbangu in order to be deported without trial. But deportation did not break the spirit of witness of these Christians. Proof of this is in their hymns:

> 'God has created Heaven and Earth.
> Nobody is more powerful than he.
> One of these days he is going to end all palaver.
> Come quickly, let us pray!'

In the former Belgian and French Congo, in Gabon, Angola and Ruanda, Kimbanguist congregations emerged, but mostly in secret. As the leaders were regularly arrested some of these groups degenerated or began endless quarrels with each other.

The latest arrests took place in 1957 (according to Ustorf 1959). Then followed the famous episode in the history of the Kimbanguist church in the sports stadium of King Baudouin, today Stadion St. Raphael. Joseph Diangienda recounted the event to Marie-Louise Martin as follows: While he stayed in the car and prayed 'a delegation of Kimbanguists went with a letter to the Belgian Governor, General Pétillon. The letter, signed by six hundred leading Kimbanguists who were known for their blameless conduct read as follows: "We are suffering too much. Wherever we assemble for prayer your soldiers arrest us. We do not want to make such trouble for the police. We will all assemble in the stadium of King Baudouin—unarmed—and there you can kill us if you want to." The alternative solution—not expressed in the letter—"or give us religious liberty".

'The delegation went to M. Pétillon while the Kimbanguists began to assemble in the Stadium Baudouin to prepare themselves for arrest and death. The governor was in a very tricky situation. "Do you believe that the government has the right to kill a whole section of the population without reason?" he asked the delegates. They answered: "Well, does the government not have this right? Why then does it have the right to deport 37,000 families?" Pétillon hesitated. He wanted to avoid a decision. What would Brussels say if he were to order the police to shoot at the unarmed crowd? What would the world press say? On the other hand, what would the *colons,* the white settlers, say if he were to concede religious freedom to the Kimbanguists? But the delegation insisted on a clear yes or no. Finally the governor did the only reasonable thing. He conceded tolerance, saying: "I concede you tolerance but without the guarantee of the government. For this I am not authorized. Yet I do not arrest you".'

'We were filled with unspeakable joy', ends Luntadila, the general secretary of the Church in his report on the incident. The negotiations still took some time. At Christmas 1959—after almost forty years wandering in the wilderness—the Kimbanguist Church was recognized by the Belgian government and put on the same level as the Catholic and Protestant missions. On 30th June 1960 Congo shook off the colonial yoke. Those Kimbanguists who had been deported—only 3,000 out of 100,000 were still alive—could return.

The Kimbanguist Church Today

The actual doctrine on Simon Kimbangu: An examination of all the passages in Kimbanguist literature which relate to Kimbangu show him as the 'envoy of Our Lord Jesus Christ', as 'prophet' and example, as the one through whom 'the people of the Congo know that God and Jesus remembered us', in one instance as the comforter promised in John 14: 12-18. The statements on the second coming of Kimbangu and his pre-existence, which a European theologian could misunderstand as christological titles, are interpreted by Marie-Louise Martin in the context of an African understanding, which—similar to that of the Orthodox church—draws together the living and the deceased Christians into one single community. The attribute 'God' is explicitly rejected for Kimbangu. The most understandable term for a European reader is probably that of an intercessor, i.e. Simon Kimbangu has a similar position in the Kimbanguist Church to that of the saints in the Catholic church. That may be due to Catholic influence. 'Yet more important is the fact that in Africa one does not approach the highest personality directly; humility does not allow it. One uses mediators . . . ' (Martin)

The hereditary princes: The church is today led by a kind of hereditary hierarchy, embodied in the sons of Kimbangu. Joseph Diangienda for instance is *Tata mfumu'a nlogon*, translated by the Kimbanguists as *chef spirituel*. It means in fact a kind of sacred supreme head or king. This hereditary religious hierarchy is often criticized by Christian theologians as being contrary to the principles of a Christian church. In this connection Marie-Louise Martin has this to say: 'We need not only educated leaders, but also charismatic leaders, in whom—as in Joseph Diangienda—something of the *exousia*, of the authority of Christ shines through. The lack of such leaders in Africa (and in Europe?) is responsible for many a crisis in the church. Africa does not live by ideas, formulas and correct confessions of faith but by concretizations, incarnations of Christian faith in the widest sense', which in my opinion does not quite explain why this charismatic quality has to be hereditary in spite of all the profound insights expressed in this statement. The problem will come up again in all its ambiguity in the next generation of leaders.

Schools, mission and social work: When the Kimbanguist children were forbidden to attend the missionary schools the Kimbanguists had to build their own schools and dispensaries. The Kimbanguist school system, which in 1968 taught 96,000 pupils in state subsidized schools and many hundreds or thousands of children and young people in schools which at that time had not been recognized, is under the leadership of F. M'Vuendy, a Kimbanguist who earned his doctorate at the Sorbonne. In addition there are schools for women, workshops for apprentices and co-operatives for farmers as well as Kibbutzim (collective farms). The Kimbanguists also build their own bridges, electricity plants and factories. A Kimbanguist evangelist has begun missionary work amongst the pygmies and shows them how to plant manioc and corn and how to raise chickens. Thus the pygmies are first given help with their economic needs in the transition from a hunting culture to an elementary agricultural culture.

In and with this social work the Kimbanguists proclaim the Gospel. They even began a mission amongst the blacks in the United States, with whom they expressed their solidarity. In one of their catechisms we read: 'Know this, that we the black race are the most dishonoured of all races whom God created in this earth. We could not finish telling the torments imposed upon us by the white man, especially the government white men. Think how we were transported by the peoples of Europe, how many blacks were put in ships like sardines in cans. Many times thousands of blacks were drowned at sea, with never a hand extended to save them. At other times a small number managed to arrive in America and other countries of the white man, but even those few fell into unlimited suffering.'

Ethics and political position: According to the church

order of 6th March 1960, the Kimbanguists follow these ethical rules:

- to respect the authorities (Rom. 13: 1-3)
- to love each other, including one's enemies (Mt. 5: 43-45)
- to abstain from strong drinks
- to abstain from tobacco and above all from drugs
- to abstain from dancing or even assisting at dances (immoral dances)
- not to swim or sleep naked
- to act with charity towards those who need it, irrespective of race or colour (Rom. 12: 9-21)
- to abstain from witchcraft
- to pay taxes (Mt. 22: 17-21)
- to avoid all back-biting against a neighbour
- to avoid all calumny against a neighbour
- every member to confess his faults to a selected body
- Kimbanguism is a church of the Holy Spirit. Therefore all the Kimbanguist Christians have to behave according to the Holy Spirit
- the EJCSK does not prohibit any food, except pork and monkey
- the church has the right to exclude a member who does not want to follow these rules.

The Church 'condemns all use of violence in trying to settle problems amongst men'. In spite of this the Kimbanguists sign on for military service. They reject capitalism and communism alike. They have successfully resisted the temptation to become the national church of Zaïre because—they say—'the church cannot be dependent on the state.'

Worship: In the Kimbanguist service the hymns, which have sometimes been created during the times of persecution, are as important as the sermon. The first historian of the Kimbanguists called their singers 'chantres'. Often the singing is accompanied by flute orchestras. Occasionally a brass band plays. Men and women share alike in the proclamation of the word. On the other hand the *chef spirituel*, Joseph Diangienda, does not preach.

He prays, for—he says—praying is more important for a religious head, for a bishop, than preaching. They meet daily in small groups for a short house-matin. At twelve o'clock they pray again. Wednesday afternoon and evening they hold short prayer-meetings. Every Saturday they meet in small prayer-groups in houses and pray throughout the night. On Sundays they celebrate their main service which—above all in Kinshasa—is extended once a month to a big festival service. At the festival service according to the African custom during a kind of stylized dance they bring their offerings: money, produce and other gifts. Without ever having read Bonhoeffer, the Kimbanguists admit no strict division between sacred and profane. The social get-together, the profane singing, making music, palavering, giving and receiving gifts has as much religious character as the 'religious' singing, praying, making music, the offertory and the stylized dancing.

The Catholicity of the Kimbanguists

Reception into the World Council of Churches: With endurance and patience the Kimbanguists tried to enter into dialogue with the European churches. That is why they wanted to enter the World Council of Churches. In the view of the Kimbanguists a Zairian church is not a church in the full sense of the word, for the church is either universal, or it is not a church at all. As the Kimbanguist church cannot be universal on its own, it considers the World Council of Churches as an instrument through which it can participate in the catholicity of the whole church—an ecclesiological insight which many European churches lack. Considerable opposition was mounted against the entry of the Kimbanguists into the World Council of Churches.

This came from two quarters: On the one hand it was

feared—and rightly so!—that the reception of the Kimbanguists into the World Council would relativize European and American missionary work in Africa. Furthermore they were not trusted theologically. They were asked to submit their confession of faith—something which never had been asked from a European or American church. But the Kimbanguist church did not have a confession of faith. Their theology is embodied in their hymns and liturgy. 'I do not have the spirit for reading', said Simon Kimbangu rightly. 'Nevertheless I have considerable intelligence for religion'. In order to please the World Council of Churches they wrote a normal evangelical confession, which was of course recognized in Geneva as a plagiarism. The submission by one of the World Council of Churches executives in Geneva that under these conditions neither the apostles, nor our Lord Jesus Christ, would ever have had a chance of being received into the World Council of Churches, remained unanswered. As the negotiations dragged on for several years, the *chef spirituel,* Joseph Diangienda, wrote an important letter to the General Secretary of the World Council of Churches on 15th July, 1969. Three points from that letter:

1. The Kimbanguist Church does not seek entry into the World Council of Churches for material advantage. She has developed independent of foreign money and she will continue to do so.
2. The reason for the Kimbanguist church's application is a spiritual one. It is high time that Christians take seriously the problems of world peace, of justice, of help to those without any rights. This is something the Kimbanguist church cannot do by herself. This task has to be undertaken by the world-wide church.
3. But if the World Council of Churches comes to the conclusion that the entry of the Kimbanguists would 'pollute' the purity of the ecumenical institution then we have to accept this with regret. But we would still like to let you know that we remain your friends.

An African Theology

The African elements in the Kimbanguist church have already been pointed out. The question is, however, whether or not the Kimbanguist church will develop a theory, a theological articulation of its practice. Perhaps this might happen in their doctrine of the sacraments. Until recently the church did not celebrate the Lord's Supper because it was of the opinion that the sacraments do not belong to one denomination even if that be the Kimbanguists. In principle the Kimbanguists argue that there are no denominational (i.e. sectarian) sacraments but only catholic (i.e. ecumenical) sacraments. 'For us', declared Joseph Diangienda to Dominique Desanti, 'communion will be more ecumenical than it is for the Catholics or the Western Protestants.' A denominational Communion contradicts the intention of Communion which is the non-rational expression of the communion of all Christians which transcends rational articulation. In the opinion of the Kimbanguists it is therefore necessary that Communion be dealt with at least within the framework of all the churches in Zaïre. In spite of this the first Communion of the Kimbanguists celebrated on 6th April 1971 was not held as an open Communion. Three hundred and fifty thousand Kimbanguists took part in a celebration which lasted for one and a half days. Instead of imported wine and bread they used: 'Honey-water; a bread made with potatoes, maize and bananas prepared in a traditional way, the banana acting as leaven.' At the moment—as in Zwingli's day—it will be celebrated only three times a year (Easter, the memorial day of the death of Kimbangu and Christmas).

So far the church does not practise baptism by water. Instead they practise spirit baptism (by a handshake, followed by raising up of the candidate who kneels before the pastor). This spirit baptism is not administered to Christians who come from other churches to the Kimbanguists. As they have already been baptized, they are simply prayed for. For children there is a ceremony of blessing.

The pastors of the church are mostly honorary and earn their own living. The problem of theological education for the present and the future pastors is therefore quite acute. Marie-Louise Martin has tackled this problem in spite of great difficulties and with great personal sacrifices. It seems that she will succeed in educating a core of African theologians who will not be alienated by their education from their social and religious milieu.

One evaluation of the church which I want to mention is the one by Geoffrey Wainwright. He measures the Kimbanguists with the yardstick of a rather strictly definable protestant orthodoxy. Not everything in the doctrine and practice of the Kimbanguists corresponds with these assumptions. In spite of this Wainwright comes to the conclusion that 'within Kimbanguism an African conception of Christ . . . may be struggling to find theological expression, and that in a potentially orthodox way.' He concedes, however, that already in New Testament times the concepts of Christ (Christ, Lord, Saviour, Son of God, Son of Man) 'came from their previous multiple background charged with associations not entirely appropriate to Jesus without transformation.' Wainwright does not seem to consider the possibility that the so-called orthodox position might perhaps not be as biblical as is generally assumed.

Marie-Louise Martin judges the chances for an 'African theology' much more positively: 'What faces us in the independent churches of Africa in general and in the Kimbanguist Church in particular is that for which missiologists in Europe have been yearning for a long time: the beginnings of a Christian theology in African cloth.'

H. W. Fehderau concludes pointedly: 'There has been much talk of making our mission churches indigenous; the Kimbanguist church *is* indigenous.' And James E. Bertsche compares the mission-based churches with the Kimbanguists: 'Against a background of a partially subsidized and largely institutionalized mission programme, there is the challenge of Kimbanguism's dynamic grassroots lay movement. Spreading along arteries of communication, across tribal lines and language barriers, its shock troops have been its enthusiastic, unsalaried laymen . . . By comparison with the effervescence of this lay movement, the average mission-established church programme must appear quite routine and unexciting indeed to the Kimbanguist.'

From this Marie-Louise Martin draws the following conclusions: 'Until now in most African theological faculties and seminaries one has taught theology according to the European pattern. Also the syllabus has been —and still is—drawn up accordingly. Of course one has translated the dogmas into African languages, and the German, French and English hymns have also been translated into the languages of the Basotho, the Zulu, the Bavenda, the Bakongo and many other people, together with the Western revival or reformation melodies. And the harmonium has also not been forgotten. But have these translations brought the Gospel to them? There is something more needed than just translation if we are really to communicate the Gospel. The Gospel and the Church should not be clothed in Western garments. Such new clothing can only be tailored by an African Church, tested through sufferings and proud of its mission. I believe that this is the case in the Kimbanguist existential interpretation of salvation-history, their hierarchy, their symbols, their rites, their African or Africanized hymns and images. That is a promising beginning. We can only

71

hope that when the Kimbanguist church has its own university-trained theologians they will not violate their heritage and speak in the Western jargon. We theologians from the West have only a small part to play in this development by explaining the historical background of the biblical texts, pointing out the *Formgeschichte*, the literary forms of biblical tradition, which have many similarities with African forms of passing on tradition. Perhaps we can also be of help when the Africans use our own terminology and do not understand it. We might also assist them in telling them how other churches have developed in other parts of the world, with special emphasis on the Early Church, the church fathers and the old African churches in Egypt, Nubia and Ethiopia, as far as we know their development. This gives us an opportunity to show where—as the case may be—wrong developments took place and why certain churches have accepted certain rites and forms. Thus we can further ecumenical understanding. Perhaps we can also assist in solving the burning ethical questions in the new Africa on the basis of a biblical theology by pointing out the dangers of a new legalism. And finally it will be our task to point continually to the cross of Christ, which is the crisis of all human undertaking, of all human desires, ideas, symbols and theologies, but where pardon, resurrection and the new creation is promised.

'I do not believe that we can do much more. We have to leave as much as possible to the Africans and be patient even when their expression, their terms, their forms, their organizations and their structures appear to us to be imperfect or even totally wrong. We have to overcome our fear of a possible syncretism, which does not mean that we close our eyes to its dangers. But it means that we trust the Holy Spirit, as Paul did, to lead the African brothers into all truth. If we acquire this attitude the day might come when Africa will produce a new formulation of the message of Jesus Christ, which might be significant for the West too and might give to the ecumenical dialogue a new dimension.

'The Gospel is a Gospel of salvation. That is exactly what Africa has perhaps understood better than the West, where we understand the word "salvation" too often as the "salvation of the soul". Salvation means in Africa that which "shalom" meant for the Hebrews: Salvation and healing—not only from infirmity, but salvation in the widest sense, "a new earth and above all, a new heaven", social justice, peace, following from this no discrimination, no bitter poverty side by side with over-whelming riches; brotherhood, order in freedom, unfolding of all potentials of life, but in such a way that the community is served, which is more important for Africans than individual fulfilment. Salvation includes healing; a new life in a new earth, free of hatred, passion, lies, corruption, oppression; and holiness as an expression of our thankfulness and the freedom which God has given in his love to all men. That will be a true eschatology . . . '

And the future?

The Kimbanguist church has experienced tremendous growth. From an elitist minority church it has grown to a mass church with three million adherents. And all that—in contrast to the European and American mission churches—without money from outside! With their own hands—but with some help from the government in respect of wages for teachers—they have built their churches and their schools. One might say: Well missions have done just the same. True, but here is a church which, out of her poverty, out of the midst of her celebration, has opened herself to the social problems of her country

73

without asking for crumbs from the rich tables of Europeans and Americans.

The wildfire development of Kimbanguism does not only imply great opportunities but also many dangers. Many questions remain open, as Dominique Desanti, who describes himself as a 'non-believer, yet profoundly interested observer', has put it. 'It might be argued, in the first place, that the strict morality and austere puritanism of Kimbanguism is running counter to present-day trends. The young people in the town, who are constantly faced with such a totally different style of life, may well prefer a more tolerant form of religion. Perhaps there's a danger that the hierarchical organization of the clergy, who are picked by the spiritual leader with no right of appeal, might tend to dampen the mystical ardour which was the strength of the early communities? Will the Church find herself forced into a certain conformity by accepting Government subsidies for schools and clinics? Finally, isn't it possible that the introduction of the Holy Communion (. . .) will put an end to one of the most original aspects of this religion, namely direct communication with God through invocation and mysticism?'

Those are questions which faced the early Christians almost 2,000 years ago, questions with which the Waldensians, the Anabaptists, the churches of the Reformation and in our century the Pentecostals, had to wrestle and which they all tried to solve in their own way, questions which focus once again on the ecumenical significance of the Kimbanguists. They expected the kingdom of God. What came was the (Kimbanguist) church. That is how Paul Raymaekers paraphrases the situation. He concludes: 'But the new church and the new society in Zaïre would not have come without this faith in a kingdom which is beyond the churches and the society.'

On another level questions arise which are similar to

those known in the European and American churches. They will be highlighted by the research of Werner Ustorf. It seems to me very likely that he can prove part of the 'official version' of Kimbanguist history to be legendary. After all the documents issued by the present leadership in Kinshasa reflect the history of their church from the orthodox (Kimbanguist) point of view. That means in historical terms: their documents reflect church history written from the point of view of the victors. That has almost always been the case—both in church and world history. What will happen if some of the historical basis of that historiography is shaken? What will happen if the diverse opinions on the 'right interpretation' of Kimbanguist history force the Kimbanguists to write their own history in dialogue with their own dissenters? Many of the more rural Kimbanguists are probably closer to traditions and values which the present leaders in Kinshasa have rejected as 'heretical'. Some of these rural Kimbanguists remained within the 'official' church, others formed their own Kimbanguist or Kimbanguistoid organizations. The battlecry 'back to Kimbangu', 'back to the times of revival', might create similar stimuli and confusions as the cry 'back to Luther, the Church Fathers or even the New Testament'. One would expect a serious questioning of ecclesiastical authority in the Kimbanguist church, both to govern the church and to decide on the right hermeneutics of their sources. That too is a problem which the Kimbanguists will have in common with other churches.

IV. The Holy Spirit and the Virgin Mary

Catholic Pentecostals

The Pentecostal Movement began almost seventy years ago as a revival movement within the existing churches. Although the Pentecostals saw themselves as an ecumenical revival movement in the established churches, they had to organize themselves very soon—with the exception of groups in Germany and France—into several larger, and a great number of smaller, free churches (so-called 'classical' or 'Historical Pentecostalism').

Since the fifties a similar Pentecostal revival has repeated itself in the Anglican and Protestant churches of the United States and in the Baptist Churches in Russia. They are called 'Neo-Pentecostals', 'Pentecostals in the Established Churches' or 'Charismatic Movement in the historic churches'. This spirituality spread very quickly too in the historical churches of both the Americas and Europe.

The rise of the Catholic Pentecostal Movement

Beginning about eight years ago a similar phenomenon can be observed in the Roman Catholic Church, and it is with Roman Catholic Pentecostalism that this chapter is mainly concerned. By 1962 there were already a few contacts between Catholics and Pentecostals in Holland and in the USA. Some priests had taken part in meetings of the Full Gospel Business Men's Association International (a lay organization within classical Pentecostalism) and thereby experienced and accepted Pentecostal spirituality but the breakthrough came only in 1966/67 when 'several Catholic laymen, all members of the faculty of Duquesne University in Pittsburg were drawn together in a period of deep prayer and discussion about the vitality of their faith . . . Not satisfied with a life of ivory-tower scholarship, they concerned themselves with the problems of the renewal of the Church . . . In recent years they had been involved with the liturgical and ecumenical movements, with civil rights, and with the concerns of world peace.'

The Ranaghan couple, both university theologians, distinguished themselves in this group of Catholic intellectuals. At the end of 1966 they read the story of the Pentecostal evangelist Wilkerson who had found prayer and the gifts of the Spirit to be the most efficacious means of combating juvenile drug-addiction. Through a report of the already mentioned neo-Pentecostal movement within Protestant churches by a journalist (Sherrill), they became curious to get to know this charismatic movement themselves. Through the mediation of the Anglican Rector William Lewis they came into contact with a charismatic prayer group. Soon they received the gift of speaking in tongues. From Duquesne the movement spread to Notre Dame University and throughout the United States. There are today over a hundred thousand Catholic Pentecostal laymen and priests in hundreds of prayer groups. The movement has spread further to Latin America, Europe and Australasia. Its literature is published in Chinese, French, Italian, Korean, Portuguese, Spanish, and other languages. The movement has ramifications which extend to the Vatican. Already there are reports of a similar development in the Orthodox churches.

In addition to the vast journalistic literature there are some scholarly publications. For a critical understanding the essays of Helder Câmara's theological research assistant Abdalaziz de Moura, of the Dominican professor of theology Lepargneur, of the British Dominican Simon Tugwell, of the lady theologian J. Massingberd Ford, the papers and documents of the 'Roman Catholic-Pentecostal Dialogue' organized by the Secretariat for promoting Christian Unity and above all of the American Benedictine Kilian McDonnell, who has examined the revival and its roots thoroughly, are indispensable. McDonnell, de Moura and Lepargneur—unlike Ranaghan and O'Connor—do not belong in the narrower sense to the Catholic Pentecostals. Therefore their critical but sympathetic approach and their exact reports are particularly to be recommended.

The relation to the classical Pentecostals

In many American cities Catholic and classical Pentecostals meet regularly for prayer-meetings. The official publications of the classical Pentecostals are not sure how to interpret this new phenomenon. That is understandable, as amongst Pentecostals until recently the Catholic church has been seen as a foreshadowing of 'the great whore'. The dialogue between Rome and Geneva was seen 'with great concern', 'because all that could lead to the uniform, worldly and anti-Christian Super-Church, which is foretold in the Revelation of John'. On the other hand Catholics have in the past produced mostly polemics against the Pentecostals based on ignorance.

All that is changing so quickly today that the members of classical Pentecostal churches cannot keep up with the changing situation. A reader from Maryland writes to the Pentecostal Evangel:

> How can the Catholics receive the Spirit and 'still go to confession and still have their idols? . . . Some of our people are going to Catholic prayer meetings and this disturbs me. As Christians we need wisdom to discern the spirits in these last days.'

Classical Pentecostals 'are "scandalized" that Catholic Pentecostals can smoke and drink and still have the baptism of the Holy Spirit'. Vinson Synon of the Pentecostal Holiness Church says that classical Pentecostals will have to make 'an agonizing reappraisal' of just what makes a Pentecostal. Nevertheless one would have to agree with Mackay who 'foresees a more cordial rapprochement between the Catholics and Pentecostals than between adherents of mainline denominations'. Rightly the Presbyterian theologian, Rodman Williams, indicates that the significance of official negotiations between Pentecostals and Catholics at the highest Vatican level 'can hardly be over-emphasized'.

Signs of a change have been apparent for some years (e.g. in the publications of the French Pentecostals). That an Italian Pentecostal church, the Chiesa Evangelica Internazionale, was introduced to the World Council of Churches by the Catholic priest Kilian McDonnell, and subsequently made an application for membership of that ecumenical institution, will even speed up this development. That is why the hitherto current polemics, of the German and Italian Catholic specialists on sects, against Pentecostalism and the corresponding condemnations of the Catholic church by the Pentecostals, will soon be obsolete.

The most important periodical of the American Pentecostals is of the opinion that the Vatican Council 'produced little worthy of note'. Yet it is obvious that a charismatic movement like the Catholic Pentecostal Movement could never have enjoyed so much freedom without the decrees of the Vatican Council. As the decree on the apostolate of the lay people underscores the necessity of charisms for the lay people, there is hardly any opposition from the hierarchy.

On the other hand in more recent Catholic publications there is an astonishing openness towards the classical Pentecostal movement, sometimes even unashamed admiration. For instance there is the speech by Lepargneur at a symposium in Sao Paulo between Protestants, Catholics and Pentecostals on 'the Holy Spirit and the Pentecostal Movement'. He began his lecture with the confession that it was not to be 'an apologetic refutation of the Pentecostal movement'. On the contrary Pentecostals have rediscovered truths which have been forgotten in the Catholic church, a point which also has been made by Tugwell.

The Pentecostals say: 'An experience is better than an argument'. In the Pentecostal miracle stories we find an attempt to provide a proof of God appropriate to an age of empirical investigation. It is easy to give a theological refutation of this proof of God, and denounce it as heretical, heathen or (if the writer happens to be protestant) at least catholic. But in my view this is to blur the problem concealed within this admittedly inadequate proof of the existence of God. The problem should be formulated somewhat as follows: In an age when all authorities are declining, the authority of preaching grows weaker every day. When the Reformation churches reply that this is the scandal of the cross, which is a stumbling block to some and foolishness to others, they are forgetting that Paul, who said this, also spoke of the cross as a power of God and that he came to Corinth 'in demonstration of the Spirit and power' (1 Cor. 2: 4).

The modern world asks such questions as: Is God alive? Is this God the Father of Jesus Christ? Is there any sense in praying and trusting this God? Is the whole business of the church simply a vast and useless enterprise run at public cost, like an elaborate religious version of Tinguely's mobiles, or at best a 'necessary illusion'? The answer the Pentecostal gives to all these questions is that of the man who was born blind: 'Whether he is a sinner, I do not know; one thing I know, that though I was blind, now I see' (John 9: 25).

On this the Dominican Tugwell comments: 'People are dissatisfied with religion that does no more than preach and moralize; they want the real thing.' In his analysis of 'The Ideology of Pentecostal Conversion', the Benedictine Kilian McDonnell aptly says that in the Pentecostal movement the problem of the 'unbelieving believer' is not met by referring him to the 'field' of abstract theological assertions in which he is hopelessly lost. He is capable neither of denying nor accepting the statements that are made about this 'theologians' God'. But—in McDonnell's view—in the Pentecostal liturgy he can experience being able to pray once again.

There is no need to point out that the Pentecostal proof of God is insufficient and in certain situations will even lead to the abolition of faith *qua* faith. To some extent the Pentecostals have seen this themselves. In spite of this there remains the question: How does faith experience the real presence of Christ? It is worthwhile for Protestants and Catholics to meditate on this question together.

The importance for the Catholic Church

Abdalaziz de Moura is attempting just such a meditation. For him the hermeneutical question does not lie mainly in the search for new words, but in the precise understanding of the significance of experience. In his excellent analysis of the Pentecostal movement he particularly emphasizes its importance for the Catholic church. He begins by asking, 'What are the possibilities and difficulties with which an ecumenical dialogue with the Pentecostals must come to grips?' He defines the Pentecostal movement as a 'conscious or unconscious protest against existing political, social, economic or religious forms'. Despite its supreme theological importance, so far no theological works have appeared— de Moura does not count polemics and propaganda as theological works—which makes the praxis of the Pentecostals (not their books!) a text for theological reflection.

As theologians have so far ignored Pentecostals, the Pentecostals, understandably enough, are not interested in theology. In any case Pentecostal theology is not carried on in rational categories but in categories of intuition and experience. The theologians, and not the Pentecostals, are to blame for this segregation because they have developed a false understanding of what academic theology is. Furthermore, de Moura continues, a false interpretation of the maxim 'No salvation outside the church' on the Catholic side has made dialogue almost impossible. 'Salvation which is exclusively bound up with the confessional formulation of one church hinders the recognition of the sovereignty of Christ', a criticism which Tugwell has also made in his own terms. Even the various Catholic and Protestant attempts at social revolution do not reach those for whom they are intended. 'They are the monopoly of a privileged élite which has access to a particular jargon'. As a result among the mass of Brazilian people the symptoms of poverty are taken as its cause. It is not surprising that the Pentecostals are not any better or any worse informed than the other churches, as the historic churches have not given any reasonable teaching for centuries. For the Pentecostals, however, the tragedy is that there is no 'popular organization' worth mentioning outside the Pentecostal denominations in Chile and Brazil.

Granted, says de Moura, the Catholic church is attempting to bring worship nearer to ordinary people by liturgical reform, but this is quite an inadequate patchwork. What has been lacking so far in all the historic churches is a *criatividade no culto liturgico*, the possibility of a liturgy in which the people play a spontaneous part, as demonstrated by the Pentecostals. As long as the Catholic church means to keep the alterations under strict control, no spontaneous new creations will arise. Even the prayer-groups and bible-groups which have arisen in slum areas are quite inadequate. The bourgeois who go to the poor and instruct them, allow themselves to be 'wondered at and reverenced by the poor' so that the presence of social superiors is a psychological hindrance to the poor in the development of their specific gifts. The Pentecostals have overcome this difficulty by having as teachers neither priests nor intellectuals nor the middle class, but poor workers like themselves. In his criticism of the Pentecostal movement, de Moura points to its obvious limitations: biblical fundamentalism, devaluation of history ('A faith which is lived outside history will not find any significance in the actual situation'), an individualism which, as a result of its disengagement from politics, acts as an upholder of the status quo.

De Moura sees the greatest danger for the future in the possible alienation of the poor once they no longer accept the comfort of their preachers, as when a worker is consoled over the death of his child with the words, 'one more angel in heaven'. On the other hand, according to de Moura an accommodation with classical theology would be 'the death of the Pentecostal Movement' and 'a betrayal of its own important insights'. Unfortunately, however, this development is precisely the one that the historic churches want to force on the Pentecostal Movement.

What other possibilities does de Moura see? Like the Lutheran theologian Harding Meyer he calls for a theology that does not begin with theory but with Pentecostal practice. The Pentecostals have brought about this practice without an ecclesiology to correspond with it. How did it come about that the Pentecostals 'developed a practice which matches the thought of the best of our theologians without their profound considerations?' Without our theoretical insights into group processes they have recognized the natural leaders of the poor community as key figures in their network of communication. That means that we, who have developed these good theories but have not put them into practice, have a great deal to learn from their method of theology, which begins with experiment.

Consequently dialogue with them must begin with the *bases populares* with *experiência e do facto concreto*. Arguments will never convince a Pentecostal that he must take political or industrial action. But if, among those engaged in politics and industrial work, he meets Christians with an authentic Christian witness instead of atheists and agnostics, he will be made to think. Arguments will never convince a Pentecostal that the return of Christ has something to do with the building of a better world. But if he comes across a missionary and a warm-hearted community of Christians whose concern is the building of a better society, that will carry conviction. Arguments will never convince a Pentecostal that he must build up solid exegetical insights. But if he meets popular evangelists who can communicate with the people and who at the same time have a positive attitude towards critical exegesis, they will lead him to re-examine his own fundamentalist position.

As a result dialogue with Pentecostals does not depend as much on our arguments as on our style of religious practice and communication. The question is whether the Pentecostal can recognize them as authentic and therefore appropriate to their subject matter.

Theological Characteristics

The Protestant Neo-Pentecostals have accepted in general the doctrines of classical Pentecostalism, in particular the doctrine of spirit-baptism with speaking in tongues (Some also their fundamentalism and ethical rigorism). But what continually gets forgotten is that in classical Pentecostalism there is already an important minority who reject this position. Among the Protestant Neo-Pentecostals who reject the fundamentalist position, one should mention A. Bittlinger, W. E. Failing and the Reformed theologian Rodman Williams. The latter tries to use the work of Bultmann, Barth, Brunner and Tillich positively, yet critically, in understanding the charisms.

In Catholic Pentecostalism the tendency is stronger to accept from classical Pentecostalism the experience but without its doctrinal articulation. For instance fundamentalism is rejected as being opposed to charisms. 'Too often in the past Christians experiencing baptism in the Holy Spirit have adopted not only the cultural environment of denominational pentecostalism but also the thought categories of the fundamentalist milieu'. Ranaghan thinks one should not be too harsh with the Pentecostals because of their fundamentalism. Perhaps it belongs to their social milieu. Yet it seems necessary for Ranaghan to interpret the charismatic dimension from different points of view, including that of critical exegesis, if the Pentecostal experience is for the whole Church and not the particularity of one sect.

From this it is concluded that charisms are not supernatural. Already the protestant theologian Arnold Bittlinger has proved that there exists no criterion by which one could judge between genuine foreign languages and speaking in tongues. 'Speaking in tongues', he says, 'must be considered as a natural phenomenon, just as dreaming, laughing or weeping'. So the 'supernatural' can be seen within an old Catholic tradition as being precisely the fulfilment of our nature.' Using functional (and not ontological) categories, McDonnell poignantly affirms: 'A gift is not a what but a how. A gift is less a new capacity and more the use of an old capacity as a function of Christ's kingdom. Quite secular activities can be gifts of the Spirit if they are used as functions of the kingdom.' Rightly Josephine Massingberd Ford asks whether Handel's 'Messiah', Bach's passions, the books of St. Thomas Aquinas are due to direct divine inspiration or human charismata. Her answer: 'An excellent combination of both'.

One of the most articulate of these charismatic Catholic theologians is the Dominican Simon Tugwell from Oxford. He has presented several meditations at the British Broadcasting Corporation, one of them including a piece of singing in tongues by three Catholic sisters which provoked several hundred letters of thanks to the BBC. It was prayerfully and meditatively prepared in the studio—of course to the dismay of the technicians who did not appreciate the purpose of this 'waste' of valuable studio time and technical facilities 'just for meditation'. The actual meditation was then done extempore.

In several publications Tugwell has defended the use of speaking in tongues which appears to him 'to mean the production of genuinely linguistic phenomena, which may or may not be identified by someone present as some definite language, but which do not convey any ordinary semantic significance to the speaker himself'. It is not simply 'praying in the Spirit', nor is it simply 'God's kindergarten'. 'Prayer that we cannot ourselves fully understand is an essential part of Christian praying: tongues is a particularly straightforward embodiment of this principle'. But it is—from a phenomenological point of view—ambiguous. That applies—says Tugwell—to all pneumatic activities. He concludes that the New Testament does not put pressure on anyone to seek the gift of tongues, but it encourages those who receive it to use it to grow into fuller and richer experience of the Christian life as a whole. Thus Tugwell suggests that this gift does have a part in the wholeness of the Christian life. 'This does not in any way commit us to accepting the Pentecostals' understanding of it, nor to their kind of religion.'

Tugwell goes on to state 'the Pentecostal doctrine is scripturally and theologically unwarrantable', and is for the theologian 'cause for alarm'. Yet he maintains that 'Pentecostalism does represent a genuine eagerness for the original, undiluted message of the Gospel which is "not in words of persuasive wisdom, but in demonstration of Spirit and power" (I Cor. 2: 4), this too makes a legitimate demand on the theologian's interest and sympathy'. He rejects the notion that the baptism of the Spirit adds anything more to Christian faith. 'Anything more than fundamental Christianity is actually less than the Gospel'.

Tugwell uses categories of medieval mysticism in order to interpret his and his fellow Catholics' spiritual experiences. Mysticism—he says 'is not intrinsically Christian, but it can be made Christian'. He differentiates between oracles and prophecy, between idols and icons. 'An idol is a god, or a manifestation of god, or an experience of god, or a doctrine of god, that one has "made a thing of".' But 'Christ is larger than his media of communication.' Prophecy and icon 'strip us down before God, peeling off our masks and pretences, our false selves', while those using oracles and idols always try to get power over God, showing thereby how right they are.

Tugwell knows of course that definitions and names (also a kind of idol) are sometimes necessary for our sanity, but they never capture God adequately. Only 'when we have overcome' (Rev. 2: 17) shall we find our full identity, will the reality of the experience of God fit its definition. That is why Tugwell sees no phenomenological difference between Christian and non-Christian mysticism, between oracle and prophecy, between idol and icon. The difference does not lie on the level of phenomenology, but on that of signification. From outside both these mysticisms look exactly alike. Only by its function, when it creates room for freedom, does it become Christian. From this Tugwell draws the conclusion that in a charismatic community there must be freedom for speaking in tongues and extempore prayer, and also freedom for abstaining from such kinds of spirituality without losing face. As among German Protestant Neo-Pentecostals, Catholic Pentecostals similarly see in community work, journalism and run-of-the-mill management, even in music, poetry and theology, charisms of the Holy Spirit.

In fairness it must be added that Tugwell is regarded with suspicion by many Catholic Pentecostals, particularly in England. They see him much more as one of their more outspoken critics than as a 'Catholic Pentecostal'. Tugwell himself, does not want to be put into that category. On the other hand he is not the only one who has misgivings about the term and the concept of the 'Baptism of the

Spirit'. It is not surprising therefore that speaking in tongues is not recognized as the 'initial sign', i.e. as the first and compulsory sign of Spirit baptism, by O'Connor. But that does not hinder Catholic Pentecostals from seeing the spiritual and psycho-hygienic value of glossolalia. The usual discarding of speaking in tongues in categories of the pathological is rejected.

It is recognized that the term 'Baptism of the Spirit' was coined by the classical Pentecostals who hardly have a theology of the sacrament. A Catholic theology of charisms should speak rather of the renewal of the Spirit received in baptism than of initiation into the life of the Spirit in a Spirit-baptism. Although Kilian McDonnell knows that among the church fathers there were some who taught 'two stages' of salvation similar to those taught in the classical Pentecostal churches, he maintains that for Paul 'becoming a Christian and receiving the Spirit occur together'.

The theologians of the Catholic Pentecostal Movement stress that Pentecostal spirituality does not hinder Catholic mariological spirituality, but, on the contrary, promotes it. In the preface to his book on the Spirit, Tugwell has even included a prayer to and with Mary. Catholics have rightly seen that the Pentecostals are—in contrast to their self-interpretation—not typically Protestant.

On the ethics of the Catholic Pentecostals one can for the time being only say that they are not rigorist and that the ecumenical contacts in the Catholic charismatic prayer-groups have kept the political aspects of a Christian spirituality alive. 'It seems to be decisive', says a Jesuit observer, 'that people who in the past could not see a black without becoming furious, can now embrace him.'

The excellent book by G. Hasenhüttl in which he describes 'Charisma' as 'the ordering principle of the

Church' does not belong in the narrower sense to our topic. Hasenhüttl, who dedicates his book 'to those who have left the church or are about to leave it', works on the basis of a very careful exegesis and, knowing the World Council of Churches' study 'The Church for Others', towards a remarkable re-ordering of the structures of the church which, according to him, should be defined from the charism (and not, as is usually the case, the other way round!). Yet in his book he never mentions the Catholic Pentecostals although they would perhaps be examples for his scholarly work.

The ecumenical significance of Catholic Pentecostals

It is still too early to make a final evaluation. However, the Jesuit G. Gispert-Sauch sees 'the important positive ecumenical value of the movement' and supposes that it might be important for a future Indian spirituality. Some indications of the ecumenical importance of Catholic Pentecostals may however be made.

The prayer-meetings of the Catholic Pentecostals shattered the 'economic-deprivation' theory that had customarily been set forth as an 'explanation' of the older, classical Pentecostalism. It was not the uneducated, but the intellectuals, not the uncritical but the critical exegetes, not frustrated Puritans but quite normal Christians who took part in these meetings. There is not only speaking in tongues but critical discussion of theological and social problems; not only the singing of hymns but the composition of hymns; not only praying, but eating, drinking and smoking. It is possible to laugh and weep, to clap hands—and also to leave the room when one does not like this style. The Jesuit Sudbrack therefore sees Pentecostal spirituality in relation to Harvey Cox's 'Feast of Fools'. Social and political topics are not excluded from their meetings. 'Any genuine movement of the Holy

90

Spirit will not stop at re-establishing unity in the family or small community or parish. It must move inexorably on towards creating freedom and justice in the larger community of the nation and among nations. Most of the participants (of the Conference at Colombia 19-23 February 1973) had worked actively in concerns of social action.' Harold F. Cohen goes even further in stating: 'One finds an interesting parallel between the charismatic renewal and the statements of the documents of Medellín'. The Mexican bishop Sergio Mendez Arceo in the review of the Full Gospel Business Men's Fellowship International in connection with the Catholic Pentecostal revival in Mexico is reported to have said: 'Only socialism can enable Latin America to achieve true development'. 'The prayer-meeting is not an end in itself, but its point is to build a mature community of Christians.' Since autumn 1971 experiments in communities' have been under way which might perhaps not only bridge the ecumenical but also the political and social divides. There was even room for a red hot revolutionary talk, which covered a condemnation of 'free trade', the revolutionary issues of the Third World, the necessity for the 'spur of Marxism' and the inevitable interlinking of economics and spirituality. These are of course important voices but they do not represent the general feelings of the rank and file Catholic Pentecostals.

The Catholic Pentecostal Movement has developed its own ecumenical momentum—an enigma both for classical Pentecostals and Evangelicals. It is true this was only possible against the background of the Second Vatican Council, but the Catholic Pentecostals have translated this into the scope of experience of the local congregation. Here *oikoumene* is not only discussed but above all lived, including its financial implications. It might be understandable that in the joy of the ecumenical discovery the theological differences between the different (protestant and catholic) churches are not taken seriously enough, as Gelpi criticizes.

In relation to the Jews (who should not be converted but be helped to become 'sanctified' as Jews) and in the situation in Northern Ireland they might perhaps make an original ecumenical contribution. The Catholics accept the fact that this revival has its roots outside the Catholic church. Though O'Connor does not allow any doubts on his Catholic orthodoxy, he answers the question whether it is thinkable that the Holy Spirit be more at work in the classical Pentecostal churches than in that church which generally has been accepted to be the most authentic church, as follows: 'This may be God's way of demonstrating to members of the Church that He alone is sovereign Lord, and that all institutions and hierarchs on earth, even in the Church, are nothing but instruments and ministers . . . We need to have it demonstrated for us that God's action transcends the action of the Church . . . '

In contrast to the Pentecostal revival sixty years ago within the Protestant churches and the occasional social disqualifications within Protestant Neo-Pentecostalism, the Bishops' Conference of the Catholic church in the USA has rather friendly relations with Catholic Pentecostalism. The Bishops say: The movement has theologically legitimate reasons for its existence and rests on a solid biblical basis. There are abuses here and there, but the movement as a whole should not be hindered. 'Prudent priests' should accompany the groups and help them to maintain the impetus which they have received from the classical Pentecostal churches without accepting their mistakes. Understandably an observer mockingly criticizes the bishops for preferring 'tamed charismatics' to the revolutionary Berrigans. Yet a much better informed specialist says that the charismatic groups and political movements like 'Black Power' are not opponents but have to be seen as belonging to the same 'movements of social transformation' (L. P. Gerlach).

Classical Pentecostals negotiate with Rome

Finally the Roman Catholic—Pentecostal dialogue is another surprise in the eventful history of the relationship between classical Pentecostals and Catholics. In contrast to the dialogue of the Secretariat for Promoting Christian Unity with the Anglican Communion or with the Lutheran World Federation this Roman Catholic—Pentecostal dialogue is not concerned 'with the problems of imminent structural union, although of course its object is with Christians coming closer together in prayer and common witness.' This mutually agreed declaration is striking in the light of the recent condemnations of Catholics by Pentecostals and Pentecostals by Catholics. It is not so long ago that Pentecostals fired at the World Council of Churches with all their guns because they suspected Geneva to be too lenient *vis-à-vis* Rome.

The Roman Catholic—Pentecostal dialogue is between the Secretariat for Promoting Christian Unity of the Roman Catholic Church, leaders of some classical Pentecostal churches and participants in the Charismatic Movement within Protestant, Anglican and Orthodox Churches. Among those participating in the dialogue one would have to mention:

from the classical Pentecostal churches: David Pu Plessis (USA), formerly general secretary of the World Conference of Pentecostal Churches; John McTernan (Italy), whose Chiesa Evangelica Internazionale has recently entered the World Council of Churches; F. P. Möller (South Africa), president of the Apostolic Faith Church; Russell Spittler (USA), president of an Assemblies of God

College; Leonhard Steiner from the Swiss Pentecostal Mission; Vinson Synon, a young historian of the Pentecostal Holiness Church (USA);

from protestant and orthodox Neo-Pentecostalism: Arnold Bittlinger, a Lutheran pastor, director of the Ecumenical Academy Schloss Craheim in Germany; Athanasius Emmert, an orthodox priest, also at Schloss Craheim; Michael Harper, an Anglican priest from England and leader of the English Neo-Pentecostals; Rodman Williams, a Reformed pastor and formerly professor at Austin Presbyterian Theological Seminary, USA;

from the Secretariat for Promoting Christian Unity: Louis Bouyer, Cong. Orat., professor at the *Institut Catholique*, Paris; Pierre Duprey, W.F., under-secretary of the Secretariat; Msgr. Balthasar Fischer, Germany; Juan Garrigues, O.P. and Albert de Monléon, O.P. from the study centre *Istina*, Paris; Jean Giblet, professor of the Catholic University of Louvain; Kilian McDonnell, Institute for Ecumenical and Cultural Research, Collegeville, Minn., USA; Heribert Mühlen, Professor of the University of Paderborn, Germany.

The documents of the dialogue show clearly the different theological starting points of the three parties, e.g. on the concept of the baptism of the Spirit. To begin with these differences were diffused by a long historical introduction into mysticism. However, David J. Du Plessis said the study of the mysticism of the past was not of particular value. 'One can find very little in ancient writings that was written by those who had the experience, and we have to rely on secondary information from those who wrote about the experience of others, yet not knowing what it was all about . . . The study of medieval charismatic phenomena through secondary sources is as futile and unrewarding as an attempt by a young man to make love to his sweetheart through the efforts of an interpreter.' As those who had experienced the Spirit, it was the declared purpose of the dialogue for the classical Pentecostals to testify to their experience. However, on the basis of his study of Catholic mysticism, another classical Pentecostal, Vinson Synon, came to the conclusion that Catholics and Pentecostals were really 'soul brothers'.

But these historical excursions were only preliminaries. The real differences appeared when the exegetical methods of biblical studies were displayed. For classical Pentecostalism the Acts of the Apostles is the normative document of the normative church. The representatives of the Secretariat on the other hand used the critical tools of biblical scholarship. That means that the latter accepted a pluralistic understanding of the Holy Spirit in the New Testament while the classical Pentecostals regarded the understanding of the Spirit by Luke as the one and only true understanding of the Spirit in the whole Bible. These differences were explicitly expressed by Bittlinger.

It is astonishing that the dialogue did not break up at this point. This was either due to the personal patience of the participants, or the art of the staff of the Secretariat in leading a dialogue, or else to the Holy Spirit being present (and perhaps these were not mutually exclusive).

More important than the results of the dialogue is the fact that it is taking place. Classical Pentecostals had always said: Pentecost is an experience, not a doctrine. However, as the Catholics have had the very same experience of the Spirit as classical Pentecostals, what does that say about the doctrine of the Roman Catholic Church? This is a difficult question for classical Pentecostalism. Originally they had expected the Catholics who had experienced Spirit Baptism to leave the Catholic Church and become members of the Pentecostal churches. And the Assemblies of God minister Wilkerson, whose report 'The Cross and the Switchblade' had won many thousand sympathizers for Pentecostalism, predicted great persecution of the Catholic Pentecostals which will force them to form a supernatural church of true believers. That means in other words: either they leave the Catholic church and become a kind of Pentecostal church or the Holy Spirit will leave them.

Such an 'either or' is impossible for the classical Pentecostals who are engaged in the dialogue. Du Plessis has therefore rejected Wilkerson's verdict and R. Douglas Wead, a former Assemblies of God minister describes in a disturbingly honest way the process of his own ecumenical education in his contact with Catholic Pentecostals. But it is very clear that a re-appraisal of the Catholic Church will lead to great tensions within Pentecostalism, just as many of the Catholic books on Pentecostalism will have to be re-written. It is impossible to tell what this dialogue will mean for the ecumenical scene in general. At the moment it seems that many Pentecostals rather harden their rejection of the World Council of Churches. One is almost inclined to believe they might say a reluctant 'yes' to ecumenical relationships with Rome and 'no' to ecumenical relationships with Geneva.

The dialogue has a political undertone which is not expressed in the documents. But it becomes clear when one takes a careful look at the list of participants. One discovers that the Latin American Pentecostals, for whom such a dialogue is of the greatest importance, are completely absent. And Africa is only represented by those churches who stand without compromise behind the Apartheid policy of South Africa. This is not necessarily a conscious political tactic. One knows from ecumenical committees how difficult it is—for financial, linguistic and organizational reasons—to get the Third World Christians to the conference table. But—this 'political innocence' is once more a highly political move. And that is true for all three parties. Miriam Castiglione, a critical observer of the Italian Neo-Pentecostal scene comes therefore to the conclusion that ecumenical Neo-Pentecostalism is an attempt to defend Christian ghettoism and to avoid the more difficult debate with non-Christians.

That is of course not confined to Neo-Pentecostals and classical Pentecostals. Pentecostals would—if Miriam Castiglione is right—just conform to the major trends in Christianity. I understand the Pentecostal leader who told me: If the Catholics come to the dialogue with their best scholars from Europe and America, why should we send the blacks? Nevertheless, I believe that in the future the classical Pentecostals would do well to invite the Pentecostal voice of the Third World, because the 'Third Force' (as Pentecostalism is called) can become a particularly appropriate channel to express the spiritual, cultural and even political aspirations of the Third World and it could be a unique interpreter between black and white, a truly 'spiritual contribution' in the biblical sense of the word. To compete with 'the best scholars from Europe and America' on a scholarly basis might be a lost battle for Pentecostals from the beginning. To understand the 'gifts of the Spirit' as the Black Pentecostals, the Mexican Pentecostals, the Kimbanguists do, might be a more important, and—in the final analysis—a more biblical approach to that dialogue.

V. The Wisdom of the Children

The Jesus People

Five years ago sociologists, journalists and theologians prophesied not only the 'death of God', but also the slow death of religion. Meanwhile we see a revival of religion of all kinds, not only in the Western, but also in the Communist world: from Indian mysticism to orgy-like drug festivals; from Protestant monastic orders to Catholic Pentecostals; from new totalitarian religions in Japan to spontaneous new churches in Africa; from Pentecostal mass meetings in the woods of Siberia to small house groups of Soviet and American intellectuals. It is evident that this religious awakening meets a human need, even if one might evaluate its multicoloured manifestations differently.

The Jesus People belong in this context. American counter-culture, the world of hippies and flower children, of drug-addicts and drop-outs, provided the background for the Jesus People. The children of the American bourgeoisie had to learn that neither violent nor non-violent protests would change the world immediately. It can, however, not be contested that the protests of the American Christians (and non-Christians) against the inhuman treatment of blacks and against the war in Vietnam changed, the political climate of the USA fundamentally. But they did not bring either peace in Asia or justice in the USA.

The young protesters were disappointed and withdrew. Asian mysticism, drugs, 'make love, not war', deafening beat, had to fill the emptiness which had been created by the disappointed hope. But this substitute for hope did not last long. What remained was a 'blue hangover', a feeling of no power, no sense, of a *misère affective*. This vacuum was filled by the new religion of which a good part 'is really a May-December marriage of conservative religion and the rebellious counter-culture'. ('Time' Magazine)

Much printed matter, little information

In spite of the avalanche of printed matter there is very little reliable information on the Jesus People. The best research was done by a team of three evangelicals. Rightly they complain that most articles which one finds in religious and church magazines are useless. 'In general', they state, 'more accurate descriptive information is provided by the secular sources than by Christian ones. Most of the Christian writers seem so eager to offer their interpretations that they have done a shoddy job of research'. Together with the report of the historian Erling Jorstad, the valuable account on the British scene by G. Corry, some information in 'Christianity Today', the two documentary volumes by Kroll and the careful but fragmentary presentations in the 'Materialdienst' (Stuttgart), one has to use the Jesus People's own publications as source material. For the rest one has to rely on personal research and patient analysis of widely disparate material.

Only estimates are available on the numerical strength of the movement. Reinhold Iblacker, who visited the centres of the American Jesus Movement in the summer of 1972, reckons that there is only a kernel of several thousand members. Enroth thinks Wilkerson's estimate of 300,000 adherents is exaggerated. Anton Schulte speaks of at least half a million and at the most of one million adherents. H. J. Geppert estimates that the million mark, the 'Spiegel' that the three million mark, has been passed. Likewise the paper 'Die Welt' speaks of millions.

Origins

The origins of the movement are also not quite clear. Several leaders claim to be the founders. It is clear that the movement did not originate within the churches and the theological colleges (e.g. in the Baptist Asbury College) although sometimes this impression is created. Similar revivals with folk-songs and rock-music are not uncommon in recent American church history. Asbury College demanded from the converts complete integration into the American middle-class culture, something which the Jesus People generally reject.

If one would rather not see the movement as originating spontaneously and simultaneously in different places, one should consider Ted Wise's small centre for healing drug-addicts (The Living Room) in Haight-Asbury, San Francisco, as the origin of the movement. At the end of 1966 Ted Wise became a Christian. Together with his friends, Steve Heefner, a disc jockey, and Jim Doop, a cigarette salesman, he discussed biblical texts with the hippies and street people of San Francisco. A number of now prominent leaders of the Jesus People movement came out of this early work.

Another birthplace of the Jesus People movement was the Pentecostal Movement, an aspect which Billy Graham sidesteps in his book 'The Jesus Generation'. David Wilkerson, a pastor of the Assemblies of God, treated drug-addicts in his 53 Teen Challenge Centres in Canada and the USA from about 1960. It is astonishing how many leaders of the Jesus People Movement came out of the Pentecostal movement. Carl Parks of the Jesus People's Army was brought up in the Assemblies of God, David Berg, the founder of the 'Children of God' was originally a director of a Pentecostal Teen Challenge Centre and had co-operated for some time with the Pentecostal Fred Jordan. Linda Meissner, originally with the Jesus People's Army, later with the 'Children of God', was formerly an associate of Wilkerson's. Susan Alamo (Christian Foundation of Tony and Susan Alamo) was, and Kathryn Kuhlman is, a well-known Pentecostal evangelist. V. P. Wierville from The Way, New Knoxville, was a Presbyterian Neo-Pentecostal. Volkhard Spitzer, the leader of the Jesus People in Berlin, was educated in the Bible School of the British Assemblies of God and is pastor of a German Pentecostal church. Peter Katz belongs to the Apostolic Church in Berlin. Jakob Zopfi and Kurt Schnyder are evangelists in the Swiss Pentecostal Mission. F. Schmutz belongs to the Swiss Apostolic Church. In many towns in Switzerland Pentecostals are leading participants in the Jesus People Movement. In most cases they offered their church buildings and chapels to be used as 'One Way' Centres.

'One of the most distinctive hallmarks of the Jesus Movement is its involvement in the Pentecostal Movement', say Enroth and his friends. It is not astonishing that 'almost all of the Jesus People are charismatics; an exception is the San Francisco Bay Area, where the influence of the non-charismatic World Liberation Front and Peninsula Bible Church predominates'. 'Many Jesus People speak in tongues.' Schulte treats in detail charismatic elements and speaking in tongues amongst the Jesus People and Kroll underscores in his translation of 'Time's' article the 'specific American features, as "speaking in tongues" and "healing through faith".'

However, it is even less possible than in the Pentecostal Movement to give a systematic catalogue of the different 'Christian Houses', the communes, the unions and separations, the organizational and friendly relations between the different groups, all the more as the situation is—as in Black Power—continually changing. The names mentioned in the bibliography have to be considered merely as signposts in the bewildering complexity of organizations and names. For historical reasons some names of centres or organizations have been included which have since disappeared or have become almost defunct.

The movement spread very quickly to Germany, Switzerland, England, Holland and Denmark. How far one can trust the reports from Morocco and Afghanistan, I am unable to judge.

It is also questionable whether one can really speak of a Jesus Movement in Sweden. It is true, however, that the leader of the Stockholm Pentecostal Filadelfia Church, Stanley Sjöberg, has introduced American Jesus People groups in Sweden. They participated in a great campaign against an alleged infiltration into Sweden by Communists. There was a violent press battle not only between Sjöberg and several leftist organizations but also within the Pentecostal and nonconformist churches. There is reason to doubt whether the Pentecostal Jesus People in Sweden have a lot in common with the American Jesus People. The American Jesus People have so far not joined the propaganda war against the Communists. On the contrary, they were known for their reluctance to be enrolled for the war in Vietnam.

Besides Sjöberg's Jesus People groups there are charismatic youth groups in the Lutheran Churches of Sweden with their own style of music and spirituality. It is an interesting mixture of modern music and high church liturgy.

The future of the movement

The religious trends in the hippie movement and the charismatic impulses of the Catholic and Wilkerson's Pentecostals form a strange mixture of hippieism and personal Christianity. How will the movement develop further? Some indications can be seen already. The Jesus People can either disappear again as they have come; or they can develop into sectarian organizations; or they might prefer some loose relationship with the established churches.

The first possibility has been shown in a number of communes and groups. The most remarkable example is 'His Place', which was founded by the famous and controversial Jesus People evangelist Arthur Blessitt. Enroth and his friends found nobody at 'His Place' except Mike Ooten, Blessitt's assistant, a fact which obviously does not hinder but rather encourages him to embark on evangelistic world tours. Enroth also found that many of the addresses of Jesus People groups or communes were incorrect. They had moved or the present residents strongly objected to being considered as Jesus People.

'Only two pieces of toilet paper, Lk. 16: 10'

The second possibility is exemplified in the history of the 'Children of God'. This group which was founded by David Berg, the former director of Teen Challenge, has developed into a highly hierarchical organization which is entirely subjected to the ruling patriarch. Berg enjoyed the support of the Pentecostal Fred Jordan for a certain time. Jordan presented the 'Children of God' in his television programme in such a way that they became attractive to right-wing businessmen who then financed

Jordan on behalf of the 'Children of God'. Yet the 'Children of God' hardly saw anything of the money, which Jordan banked, but that did not trouble them because they are indifferent to money. Compared with the value of the invaluable souls they had won during their stay at Jordan's ranch and who were prepared to come with them, what did a $40,000 loss of investments in the ranch matter? Money, prestige, education 'is all just shit in their eyes'.

They protest against Nixon's 'Fourth Reich' which they see as analagous to the Third Reich. That is why they emigrate from the United States to Europe. Oddly enough they also discovered the World Council of Churches in Geneva for whom they have a lot of sympathy, but they have no sympathy for the churches. That is why 'all the famed reformers, world-changers, pioneers, martyrs and other young radical revolutionaries were rebels against the rotten, decadent, decrepit, hypocritical, self-righteous, inflexible, affluent, self-satisfied, proud, stubborn, disobedient, blind, blood-thirsty, Godless, dead, selfish, churchy, unchangeable older generation of their day'. The 'Children of God' have a 'revolutionary music' and 'no organ lullabies for the dead'.

They hold all goods in common. Their discipline is hard. Men with long hair are sometimes asked to cut it and others with short hair might have to grow it long. On the door of the toilet at their centre in Essen one can read: 'This is a revolution. Use only two pieces of toilet paper, at the most four! Luke 16: 10. Redeem the time. Repeat bible verses, pray!' In their eyes it is not enough to abstain from drugs. Those who are saved have to develop 'a completely new life-style'. And that is exactly what they can learn with the 'Children of God'. As one might expect, they are deeply suspicious of the other Jesus People. Likewise the 'more established' Jesus People leaders reject the 'Children of God'. The King James translation is the only Bible which they accept. So they state quite categorically: 'About 6,200 years ago God created the universe in six days'. Their methods of evangelism are at least unorthodox, if not violent, which led to a Member of Parliament in England unsuccessfully urging the Home Secretary to deport the American leaders. Kenneth Frampton, one of their former supporters, was so disillusioned that he published a booklet 'Beware the Children of God'.

Repeating a well-known prophecy from Pentecostal circles which foretells that California will soon sink into the ocean, they are moving towards an apocalyptic future. All other Christians will at the time of the anti-Christ accept the sign of the beast. Some might then recognize that only the 'Children of God' are really children of God.

The 'Children of God' have already founded 137 colonies in forty countries (including Australia, Austria, Belgium, Costa Rica, Cyprus, Denmark, Egypt, England, Germany, Greece, Guatemala, Holland, Italy, Jamaica, Japan, - New Zealand, Norway, Mexico, Peru, Puerto Rico, South Africa, Spain, Sweden, Switzerland, Thailand, Turkey, Venezuela). They claim 2,343 committed full-time members. They win the stronger and more serious adherents of the other Jesus People groups, as, for example, Linda Meissner and David Hoyt. Because Hoyt was disgusted by the superficial spirit of the Jesus Movement he joined the 'Children of God'. According to him, the charismatic and Jesus Movement had already been corrupted in their first five years of popularity. He rejected the watered-down Gospel of the Jesus People and accepted the hundred per cent Christianity of the 'Children of God'.

The closest parallel to the 'Children of God' within the

Pentecostal Movement can be seen in the 'Latter Rain Movement' and in John Alexander Dowie's revival movement. At the beginning of this century Dowie founded the communist-Christian city of Zion in Illinois and its branches in Holland, South Africa and Switzerland. A great number of Pentecostal leaders came from these early Zion churches.

The 'Children of God' practise an 'all or nothing' religion. Enroth affirms that 'the majority of the "Children of God" are genuine converts to Christianity, however eccentric and harmful the aberrations present in their thought and practice'. He states, and proves with ample quotations, that there is, however, only one step from Watchman Nee to the 'Children of God'.

The periodical published by the charismatic renewal in England comes to an entirely different conclusion: 'It is a mistake to think that the next move lies with the "Children (of God)"—that they must come into the churches. That is the same mistake that the churches have been making in regard to the unbelievers—waiting for them to come'.

The psychological evaluation of the Jesus People by the Swiss psychologist Willy Canziani is in my opinion particularly accurate in relation to the 'Children of God'. Canziani mentions the 'psycho-hygienic relevance of the group' and describes their spirituality as follows: 'The kingdom of God is not a kingdom of the future. It is here already in the community of love of the Jesus People . . . Jesus People do not proclaim an old or a new truth. They do not announce religious revival. To a great degree they experience together the happiness of a redeemed world. Transcendence is replaced by personal happiness, by the immanence of the group experience. In this respect the Jesus People are nearer to the hippies than to the churches . . . '

A New Ecumenical Movement?

The third possibility is for the Jesus People to develop a critical rapprochement with the established churches. This is happening now either in the form of denominational youth organizations or in co-operation with local churches, in Germany and Switzerland often in relation to existing local Pentecostal congregations. The German bishop, Kurt Scharf, and other representatives of the German Established churches also consider the Jesus People Movement as a 'fundamentally Christian movement'. The Archbishop of Canterbury, the Pope, Cardinal Alfrink and former Vice-President Agnew also made positive statements about the movement.

In America, Blessitt had some difficulties in placing his converts in the existing churches. 'In a survey some pastors bluntly told Blessitt they didn't want blacks or anyone with a hippie background in their churches. Nearly fifty others said they were "willing" but begged off because they "lacked a church programme that would interest those young people" . . . Most of our people want to share their Christ with the hippies, but not their pews—until the hippies conform to "straight" appearances.' On top of this, many of the new converts do not see anything wrong in Marijuana. 'Most eventually abstain, but for unorthodox reasons.' They say, 'Who needs drugs when they have a permanent high with Jesus? Christians must obey the laws, even bad ones'.

In spite of this there are churches, for example the Hollywood Presbyterian Church, which are not only ready to accept hippies into their churches, but also to finance the Hollywood Free Press, even if theologically they do not agree with its content. One of the pastors of this church, Don Williams, describes how he was introduced by a girl named Cheryl into the world of the hippies. By chance she attended one of his services and decided to

107

become a Christian. Williams taught her to pray but she taught him something about himself. 'One week after I met her', he writes, 'she came again to church, rushed across the patio, threw her arms around me and gave me a big kiss. For a young, unmarried minister who had avoided any hint of scandal, I was stunned. I felt as if my head were turning 360 degrees looking for the church's elders, while every muscle in my body froze. Later in reflection on this incident I realized that Cheryl was only being her street self. I further realized that while I talked about Christian freedom, Cheryl actually was much more free than I. It was a new world indeed that I was entering'.

The new world was the world of hippies, of drug-addicts, of pop-culture. Williams came into contact with the people from this new world and many of them found a new purpose in their lives through his ministry. The Bible became an important book and they helped each other in their daily life. Don Williams also received help. He realized the importance of music in that culture—'It is to the musicians, then, that we must look to understand the form and content of the youth culture. The musicians are its prophets, priests, and kings. As priests they offer communion. As kings they conquer and rule. At Wood-stock we were treated to the spectacle of a twentieth-century pilgrimage to Jerusalem, the Holy City, where the priests made their musical sacrifices on the high altar before an awed congregation.'

Duane Pederson describes what happened at Calvary Chapel when the hippies began to fill it. 'Already after a few weeks the church was packed full. The people sat on the floor and on the steps of the altar. Finally one guy of the old establishment came along and complained. The studs of the blue jeans might scratch the pews and the costly carpet might be soiled by the naked and dirty feet.

One Sunday morning Chuck (the pastor) brought the matter into open discussion. He said: "O.K., put the pews out and roll the carpet up. But the people stay here!" ' In contrast to Schulte, who sees in the Jesus Movement fundamentally a 'movement within the American church establishment', Pederson says, 'The church must decide. For it is the church—not the young people—who is at the cross roads. And now the question for the church is either to take Jesus seriously or to shut up shop.' And the Anglican principal of a theological college, Michael Green, adds, 'The young people have found Christ. But not the Christ of the churches. The churches have tamed him and domesticated him. The churches seem afraid to talk about him . . . '

On the other hand Helmut Aichelin finds 'the attempts to incorporate the movement into traditional forms of worship and spirituality almost depressing. It is in this way that the thinking of yesterday takes the upper hand and sees itself justified by the attendance of these young people. However, so far they have not lost all of their original freshness'.

For the leader of the German Jesus Movement, Volkhard Spitzer, 'the ecumenical dimension is vital'. The Swiss Jesus People Paper also alluded to this: 'The 16th century brought unfortunately a split within Christianity and the 19th century brought new religious battles and misfortune and scandals. We confess the same Lord. We have entered a Christian community of faith by the same baptism and yet we do not pray together. Sunday after Sunday the believers go to church in order to pray at the same time to the same God—only separately. It is the desire and the hope of today's Christians, that God might restore the visible unity of all the believers.' Many observers have also drawn attention to this ecumenical spirit in the movement. Jews, Catholics, Protestants and even those with no particular religious beliefs are to be found amongst them. 'The Jesus People are of ecumenical importance, however one interprets that word', says the Dutch churchman Albert van den Heuvel. 'They are international, travelling from continent to continent, sprouting simultaneously in Australia and Austria, Germany and Germantown. Like the whole Christian Church they are more numerous in the North Atlantic community, but they are not without ambassadors and peers in the "two-thirds world". Jesus People do not heed denominational differences; for them the people of God are one and undivided. They form a cross-denomination community, attracting criticism and praise across all the confessional lines. They are ecumenical in the sense that they regard the unity and renewal of the people of God as their first platform line. Some groups hold a sweeping, though not unprecedented, concept of ecumenism simply declaring themselves the only true church; others are more cautious, describing their experience as meant for the whole church and available to everybody. A strong missionary commitment is balanced by an emphasis on liturgy and even on the renewal of society. Their concept of mission is modern: a bold statement of the Gospel in contemporary language, no emphasis on having to join the missionary's church. Through their care for peers they show a deep commitment to what in the international debate is called "humanization". Their celebrations are fiercely indigenous but usually rather "orthodox" in sacramental forms and use of the Bible. The renewal of society comes through the changed individual and not by confrontation between their community and the whole of society. Here they remind us more of the European revival movement *Réveil* in the 19th century than of the Social Gospel Movement or the Life and Work Movement. But it is all there.'

Attempt at an Assessment

Assessment is controversial. From a marxist or sectarian point of view the movement is flatly rejected, condemned as the 'last cry' or as the manipulation of clever religious business men or in an uncritical way taken as proof of the validity of an evangelical old-time religion.

Thus it is all the more astonishing that the Evangelicals have published several critical assessments. Enroth, Ericson and Peters point to their anti-intellectual, anti-cultural and anti-institutional attitude, which wants to by-pass every problem with the slogan 'Jesus is the answer'. Unbelievers are sometimes considered less as persons than as potential converts. 'Getting Jesus' peace into one's heart may be the best single contribution which an individual can make toward world peace, but it is not sufficient by itself. Even if everyone in the world became a Christian, it is doubtful that peace would "take care of itself".' Albert Springer, a German Evangelical, sees enough evidence of its dangerous and deceptive character in the connection between Jesus People and the Pentecostal evangelist Wilkerson. According to Springer, Jesus People belong to those 'that work iniquity' (Mt. 7: 23). Similarly James Rayne speaks of a 'strong delusion'.

Many call for instruction for the Jesus People. Only there is no agreement about the content of such instruction. For the Reformed the Jesus People are not reformed enough, for the Adventists not adventist enough. For the Pentecostals they are not puritanic enough and for the leader of Campus Crusade they speak too much in tongues. The German evangelist Anton Schulte 'could hardly grasp that those long-haired guys could be as Christian as the "straight" young people just sitting beside them'. However, in the course of his dialogue with the Jesus People, he was enlightened on this point. In this case the Jesus People instructed the evangelist!

111

The evangelical researchers point to a serious problem which arises when Jesus People get hooked on drugs again or when they forsake their religious community for other reasons. These young people are now immune to the Gospel. 'There is no anti-christian like an ex-Jesus person.' Yet the same evangelical researchers also state clearly that the Christian communes are a highly remarkable attempt at finding a revolutionary alternative to our bourgeois style of life.

Some recognize in the Jesus People Movement a challenge to the churches. We have to recognize that the 'power for fellowship decreases in institutionalized religion and increases in the spontaneous, free religiosity'. The young generation 'participates in a religious underground, which looks to us like a jungle, albeit hidden under the concrete cover of a seemingly rationally dominated world'. In his essay on 'Integration of emotions into the experience of faith', Siegfried Scharrer avoids a cheap 'as well as' and states in the tradition of the reformation: 'The Holy Spirit moves "in, with and amongst" linguistic, sociological and psychological approaches'. That means that phenomenological categories are unsuitable for assessing the work of the Holy Spirit. And even if one suspects some pagan forms in the movement, one will have to agree with Andrew M. Greeley—'Even if it is paganism, it is at least good paganism.' 'Through the medium of pop-culture the new religion imitates the images of classical religions and at the same time develops forms of a wild, almost archaic religion, which springs out of the yearning for transcendence.' In paraphrasing a quote of Geppert one could say, only a church which again incorporates the dimensions of paganism, 'a Church which learns, not to satisfy the desire for myths, but which helps to overcome it, a Church which accepts that emotions and play have a

112

place in religion . . . , a Church which knows that it is part of the secular world and therefore does not build sacred islands, such a Church could perhaps communicate with the young people who flee from its worship to "Children of God".' There is no point in rejecting the forms of ecstatic spirituality—either with condescending wit or with shocked indignation—rather we have to 'understand' what ecstasy is. And even if there are pathological people among them one would have to agree with Gerhard Adler that 'God is also a God of the neurotics'.

The reports on race relations are conflicting. Obviously there is no active race barrier among the Jesus People, but the photographs and the reports make it clear that the Movement is a product of the affluent society of the West. No white church really has a right to criticize this. As a member of the Jesus Movement rightly observed, 'Why do church people always draw their own portrait when they criticize others?'

Other observers see in the Jesus Movement a flight from reality, a new drug. In order to avoid the real problems, the Jesus People replace the deadly chemical opium by a less dangerous religious one. The Swiss journalist Yves Bebié says, 'Truly fundamental changes in society are brought about by those who read the holy scriptures (be they Marxist or Christian) critically and seriously'. To this one would like to object that thorough criticism does not automatically create a new hope. Only if drug-addicts experience that prayer unhooks them from the drugs, do they take courage. It should not be overlooked that the religious treatment of drug-addicts claims to have only 20% failures while the secular institutions have to accept 99% failures. A lazy man, a drug-addict, a desperate will never be 'converted' by arguments. Only if he has tangible experience of hope will he be ready to reflect critically and seriously on the opportunities and the limits of this new hope. Yet if he avoids critical reflection then even a genuine experience of hope might degenerate into a shallow emotionalism or a fixed ideology.

In his cautious evaluation of the political aspect of the Jesus Movement, the historian Erling Jorstad emphasizes a point of view which has been overlooked so far. He observes a fundamental difference between earlier revivals in America and the Jesus People revival. 'The great revival preachers of the past never seriously challenged the American love affair with free enterprise . . . On every level of today's new-time religion we find a massive indifference, and often a marked hostility, towards these older attitudes. Communal living is practised by many of the teen-age and rural Jesus people . . . ' 'No concept of personal property could be further from the convictions of Moody, Sunday or Graham' than the one held by Jesus People. Furthermore, the students among the Jesus People show a far deeper concern for such complex and massive contemporary problems as war, racism, pollution, and poverty, than did earlier evangelicals. In general the Jesus converts did not support the war in Vietnam, and indeed, they encouraged resistance to the draft. Some even refuse to salute the American flag. Pointedly, but somewhat sweepingly, 'Time' Magazine sums up the situation as follows: 'Liberals resent their insistent orthodox theology, conservatives their communal life-style.'

The evaluation by the Pentecostal churches of the Jesus People Movement is important. At the beginning and above all in the USA, Germany and Switzerland, the Pentecostals praised the new movement greatly. Today, however, the American Pentecostals, who acted as a kind of midwife to the new movement, look rather confused—just like that hen who had hatched out ducklings and discovered later that the new 'chickens' were able to swim. Wilkerson stands nervously on the shore and shouts to the new Christians—To be a Christian means to cut your long hair, to conform to a decent American style of life and to give up opposition to our foreign policy—a pointer to the fact that the American Jesus People Movement is not wholly a-political. The unorthodox language and the less rigorous rejection of drugs in some Jesus People groups, prompted Wilkerson to denounce them publically. This was followed by a statement by one of his Teen Challenge directors, who regretted Wilkerson's authoritarian methods. There is also dissent in relation to what is proper for a Christian in the realm of music. The attacks on jazz and Beat in Pentecostal publications are still reverberating. Jakob Zopfi called it 'coughing music', Wilkerson 'the devil's heartbeat' and the British Pentecostals heard in it 'the covetous moans of a lost generation, unable to fill its vacuous soul with the toys that bring no true salvation'.

The German Pentecostals are more generous. The hippie outlook does not bother them. The director of their Bible school, Ludwig Eisenlöffel, is of the opinion that the Pentecostals are so far the only denomination in Germany which allows the Jesus People to hold public meetings in their chapels. This in spite of the Jesus People's ecumenical leanings and their undogmatic religion which the Pentecostals consider as an elementary weakness to be overcome in the future. It is therefore possible to describe the Jesus Movement in Germany as an emancipatory movement among pietistic Pentecostal youth who have at last found a rationalization for a style of life hitherto forbidden them by their ecclesiastical leaders. But there is no indication 'that in West Germany the Jesus Movement has exercised any lasting influence on the young generation as a whole'. Also in England,

Scandinavia and Switzerland there are no signs of a 'Jesus revolution'.

For myself, I do not think that it is possible to make a general evaluation of the movement as a whole. One can only evaluate specific groups in the different geographical areas. Much reminds me of my own youth. Then, night after night, I also read the Bible (in Luther's old translation). Daily I expected the Lord's coming in the clouds and I preached the Gospel to anyone I could get hold of. I used all my free time for prayer, for singing Christian hymns and for public witness. It is true that there came a time when I had to admit to myself that faithful witness demanded a more solid foundation than a burning desire to evangelize one's fellow-men. (However, I do not want to imply that this will necessarily be everybody's experience.) At the same time I discovered that literature and the arts are not just the works of the devil and that the Holy Spirit also moves outside the Bible and the 'communion of the saints'. After all it is the well-known Pentecostal leader, David J. Du Plessis, who time and again has emphasized that according to Acts 2: 17 the Holy Spirit is 'poured out on all flesh' (and not on the Christians alone). In a recent talk Du Plessis describes how—as a young man—he considered himself to be 'the Lord's smartest, best, public prosecutor', how he prayed to God that he might preach his theological antagonists 'under conviction'. He wanted to see the Pentecostal movement 'blanket' the world. 'I am thankful', he says, 'that the Lord delivered me from my sectarianism.' And he goes even so far as to see the Spirit at work not only in the traditional churches, amongst the ecumenicals, orthodox, catholics and liberals, but even in the secular world. 'I maintain', he writes, 'that the Holy Spirit is more active and often gets more consideration and recognition outside of the church than inside.'

It is therefore no wonder that we find signs of the Spirit in unexpected places. It may be that this insight hinders a direct and aggressive evangelism. I do not want to play off one style of spirituality against another. 'The Jesus People in fact present us once again with the request for more pluriform structures in the churches. It is no good mixing Jesus People with our ordinary congregations. What is needed is recognition, acceptance and critique: the elements of a true friendship or, to use fashionable language, of true dialogue.' (v.d. Heuvel)

Perhaps certain criteria could be agreed upon for this dialogue (1 Cor. 14: 29). For example: This religion is by itself neither good nor bad, neither Christian nor pagan. It becomes good if it is used for the healing of our sick world, and Christian if it accepts mutual criticism in ecumenical fellowship. It becomes un-Christian if it absolutizes its religious or para-psychological experience and evil if it enslaves people, insists on obedience to a new law and makes them dependent.

Where are the Jesus People today, two years after the so-called Jesus revolution? It is part of the wisdom of the children it seems to me that children grow up. They may retain some of their insights, lose and modify others. What remains is what they remember of their youth. It would not astonish me in five or ten years time to find pastors and evangelists, and also prominent lay people in different churches, who will tell me: 'You know in 1972 I walked behind Arthur Blessitt when he carried the cross through the Midlands. That is where I became a Christian.' Or: 'At that youth festival in Germany, for the first time in my life I realized what it meant to be a Christian.' However, I fear that there will be many more who will say nostalgically, 'Yes, once I was a Christian when I came into contact with the Jesus People . . . Those

117

were the days of my youth. It is all over now.' And there is a third possibility that in a few years time conventicles may still be found meeting regularly every fortnight, trying to live on the memories of a past when they made headlines in the newspapers.

Bibliography

On Chapter 1: A Kite Flies Against the Wind

Charles G. Adams, 'Some Aspects of Black Worship', *Journal of Church Music*, Febr. 1973, 2-10 (reprinted from *Andover Newton Quarterly*, Jan. 1971).

Assemblies of God (ed), *Our Mission in Today's World. Council on Evangelism. Official Papers and Reports*. Springfield, Mo.: Gospel Publ. House, 1968.

David B. Barrett, *Schism and Renewal in Africa. An analysis of six thousand contemporary religious Movements*. Oxford UP, 1968.

— 'Ad 2000: 350 Million Christians in Africa', *Int. Review of Mission* 59/233, Jan. 1970, 39-54.

Frank Bartleman, *What Really Happened at Azusa Street?* ed. John Walker. Northridge, Calif.: Voice Christian Publ. Inc., 1962.

David M. Beckmann, 'Trance: From Africa to Pentecostalism', *Concordia Theological Monthly* 45/1, Jan. 1974, 11-26.

Alexander A. Boddy, 'Ueber Land und Meer', *Pfingstgrüsse* (Mülheim/Ruhr) 1912/13 (originally published in the British Pentecostal periodical *Confidence*).

Dietrich Bonhoeffer, 'Bericht über den Studienaufenthalt im Union Theological Seminary zu New York', in: *Gesammelte Werke*, (Munich: Kaiser-Verlag) I, 1958, 84-103.

Arthur M. Brazier, *Black Self-Determination. The Story of the Woodlawn Organization*. Grand Rapids: W. B. Eerdmans Publ. Cy. 1969.

— 'The Origin of the New Testament', *Christian Outlook* (Pent. Assemblies of the World, East Orange, N.J.) 39/4, April 1962, 3.

Malcolm J. Calley, *God's People. West Indian Pentecostal Sects in England*. Oxford UP, 1965.

Church of God in Christ, *Charter of Incorporation and Constitution of the Church of God in Christ*, no place, no date (Church of God in Christ, Memphis, Tenn., 1922).

— *History and formative years of the Church of God in Christ*, with excerpts from the life and works of its founder, Bishop C. H. Mason, reproduced by J. O. Patterson, German R. Ross, Julia Mason Atkins. Memphis, Tenn.: Church of God in Christ Publ. House, 1969.

Church of the Living God. *Glorious Heritage. The Golden Book. Documentary-Historical*, commemorating Diamond Jubilee Year 1889-1964, no place, no date (St. Louis, Mo.: Church of the Living God, 1964).

James H. Cone, 'Black Spirituals: A Theological Interpretation', *Theology Today* 29/1, April 1972, 54-69.

R. C. Cunningham, 'Social Concern Articulated', *Pentecostal Evangel* (Springfield, Mo.) no. 2840, 13.10.1968, 5.

George Dugan, 'Mass Evangelism Called of No Relevancy to Blacks', *New York Times*, 5.4.1970.

R. L. Fidler, 'Pentecostal History Lends Important Role to Blacks', *The International Outlook*, 4th Quarter, 1971.

Miles Mark Fisher, *Negro Slave Songs in the United States*. New York: Citadel Press, 1953.

Luther P. Gerlach and Virginia H. Hine, *People, Power Change. Movements of Social Transformation*. Indianapolis and New York: Bobbs-Merrill Cy. Inc., 1970.

Morris E. Golder, *History of the Pentecostal Assemblies of the World*. no place (M. E. Golder, Indianapolis, Ind.), 1973.

Michael Harper, 'Question of Colour', *Renewal* (London) no. 15, June/July 1968, 2f.

Virginia H. Hine, 'Pentecostal Glossolalia. Toward a Functional Interpretation', *Journal for the Scientific Study of Religion* 7/2, 1969, 211-226 (Bibl.).

Walter J. Hollenweger, *Kirche, Benzin und Bohnensuppe. Auf den Spuren dynamischer Gemeinden*. Zürich: Theol. Verlag, 1971.

— 'Spirituals', in: G. J. Davies (ed), *A Dictionary of Liturgy and Worship*, London: SCM, 1972, 349f.

— 'Pentecostalism and Black Power', *Theology Today* 30/3, Oct. 1973, 228-238.

— *Black Pentecostal Concept*. Concept no. 30, Geneva: WCC, June 1970.

M. McGregor Jones, *A Slave Becomes Organizer. A True, Authentic Story of Mother Lizzie Robinson's Life As Taken From Her Own Lips.* New Orleans, La.; M. McGregor Jones, no date.

Ozro T. Jones, 'Our Pentecostal Opportunity in This Hour of Religious Crisis', in: D. Gee (ed), *Fifth World Pentecostal Conference, Toronto.* Toronto: Testimony Press, 1958, 149-160.

W. H. Judd, 'Political Action Should Be By Christians, Not By Churches', *Church of God Evangel* (Cleveland, Tenn.), 53/24, 19.8.1963, 23.

Leonard Lovett, *Perspective on Black Pentecostalism,* unpubl. paper 1972.

— *Pentecostal-Holiness Bibliography.* Atlanta, Ga.: C. H. Mason Theological Seminary, 1973.

A. and M. Mitscherlich, *Die Unfähigkeit zu trauern. Grundlagen kollektiven Verhaltens.* Munich: Piper & Co., 1970.

S. O. Osoba, 'Fascinating But Largely Speculative', *Orita, Ibadan Journal of Religious Studies* 4/1, June 1970, 64-69.

J. O. Patterson (ed), *Holy Convocation Church of God in Christ* 1969. Memphis, Tenn.: Church of God in Christ Publ. House, 1969.

Pentecostal Assemblies of the World, 1963 *Minute Book of the Pentecostal Assemblies of the World,* no place, 1963.

Charles H. Pleas. *Fifty Years Achievement (History). Church of God in Christ,* no place, no date (Memphis, Tenn.: Church of God in Christ Publ. House).

Th. Spörri (ed), *Beiträge zur Ekstase* (Bibl. Psych. et Neur. 135) New York and Basel: S. Karger, 1968.

Vinson Synan, *The Holiness-Pentecostal Movement in the United States,* Grand Rapids, Mich.: W. B. Eerdmans Publ. Cy., 1971.

James S. Tinney, 'Black Origins of the Pentecostal Movements', *Christianity Today,* 8.10.1971, 4-6.

Lawrence Williams, 'First Century Pentecost', in: D. Gee (ed), *Sixth Pentecostal World Conference, Jerusalem* 1961. Toronto: Testimony Press, 1961, 45-50.

L. Zenetti, *Heisse (W) Eisen. Jazz, Spirituals, Beatsongs, Schlager in der Kirche.* Munich: Verlag J. Pfeiffer, 1966.

On Chapter II: Flowers and Songs

Maria Josefina Amerlinck y Assereto, *Ixmiquilpan: un estudio comparativo de evangelistas y católicos* (Anthropological thesis, Universidad Iberoamericana, Mexico, 1970, dupl.).

Benno M. Biermann, *Las Casas und seine Sendung. Das Evangelium und die Rechte des Menschen.* Mainz: Matthias-Grünewald-Verlag, 1968.

Códice Matritense de la Real Academía (textos en náhuatl de los indígenos informantes de Sagahún), ed. facs. de Paso y Troncoso, Madrid, fototipía de Hauser y Mente, VIII, 1906.

Archie R. Crouch, 'A Shoot Out of the Dry Ground: The most rapidly growing Church in Mexico', *World Outlook*, April 1970, 33-35.

Arnulfo Espinosa, 'Datos para la historia de la Uníón de Iglesias Evangélicas Independientes', *Mensajero Pentecostés* (Pachuco, Hgo), 2/60, Jan. 1961, 9-11.

— 'Cinco años de unificación', *Mensajero Pentecostés* 2/61, Febr. 1961, 3-8.

Maclovio L. Gaxiola, *Historia de la Iglesia Apostólica de la fe en Cristo Jesús de México.* Mexico, D.F.: Librería Latinoamericana, 1964.

Manuel J. Gaxiola, *La serpiente y la paloma. Análisis del crecimiento de la Iglesia Apostólica de la fe en Cristo Jesús de México.* South Pasadena, Calif.: William Carey Library, 1970.

Felicitas D. Goodman, *Speaking in Tongues. A Cross-Cultural Study of Glossolalia.* Chicago and London: University of Chicago Press, 1972.

— 'Apostolics of Yucatán: A Case Study of a Religious Movement', in: Erika Bourguignon (ed), *Religion, Altered States of Consciousness, and Social Change.* Columbus: Ohio State U.P., 1973, 178-218.

Venancio Hernández, 'Hombres nuevos—sociedad sana', *Estudios ecuménicos* (Mexico) 1969/2, 1-10.

Walter J. Hollenweger, 'Flowers and Songs', *Int. Review of Mission* 60/238, April 1971, 232-244; also in German (*Ev. Theologie* 31/8, Aug. 1971, 437-448), Spanish (*Concept* no. 32, Oct. 1970) and Italian (in: R.La Valle (ed), *Le chiese e la guerra,* Rome 1972, 141-155).

— *Concepto Latinoamericano III,* Concept, Special Issue 32, Oct. 1970 (Geneva, WCC).

Las Casas, *Opúsculos, cartas y memoriales,* ed. J. Pérez de Tudela Bueso, Madrid 1958 (Biblioteca de Autores Españoles 110).

— *Apologia,* Ms. in the Bibliothèque Nationale, Paris, Nuevos Fondos Latinos 12.926. Biermann announces its imminent publication (Biermann, *Las Casas,* 43).

B. Guadalupe Láscari, 'Josefina Láscari', *Mensajero Pentecostés* 3/9, June-July 1964, 13f.

Walter Lehmann, *Sterbende Götter und christliche Heilsbotschaft. Wechselreden indianischer Vornehmer und spanischer Glaubensapostel in Mexiko, 1524. Spanischer und mexikanischer Text mit deutscher Uebersetzung.* Stuttgart: W. Kohlhammer, 1949.

Miguel León-Portilla, *La filosofía náhuatl, estudiada en sus fuentes.* Mexico: Universidad Nacional, 1963; English: *Aztec Thought and Culture. A Study of the Ancient Nahuatl Mind.* Oklahoma; University of Oklahoma Press, 1963.

Mensajero Pentecostés 2/62, March 1961, 20 (on persecution of Pentecostals).

— 2/63, May 1961, 25: El Cardenal José 'Efrain' Garibi Rivera (quoted from *Rototemas* 6.12.1958).

Martin Niemoeller, 'Nochebuena', *Mensajero Pentecostés* 3/6, Jan. 1964, 3-5 (Sermon of Niemoeller in Mexico and mention of 'El hombre que se enfrentó a Hitler' by Pedro Gringoire, Mexico 1938).

T. L. Osborn, 'Preguntas y respuestas', *Mensajero Pentecostés* 3/8, April-May 1964, 6-8.

Andrés Ornelas, 'Libertad y patriotismo!' *Mensajero Pentecostés* 2/80, Sept. 1962, 5-6.

Antonio Peñafiel, *Cantares Mexicanos,* Ms. de la Biblioteca Nacional, Copia fotografica, Mexico, 1904.

Raymundo Ramírez, *Bodas de Oro. Movimiento de la Iglesia Cristiana Independiente Pentecostés.* Pachuco, Hgo: Iglesia Cristiana Independiente Pentecostés, 1972.

— El pastor evangélico Hilario Aragon brutalmento asesinado, *Mensajero Pentecostés* 2/72, Jan. 1972, 24f (quote from *Pensamiento liberal,* 15.11.1961).

W. R. Read et al., *Latin American Church Growth.* Grand Rapids, Mich., 1969, 165-169.

Jacques Soustelle, *La vie quotidienne des Aztèques à la veille de la conquête espagnole.* Paris: Hachette, 1955.

Theo Tschuy, Lateinamerika im Umbruch, *Der Wanderer von Land zu Land* (Basel) 37/1, 1963, 1-4.

On Chapter III: Pentecost of N'Kamba

E. Andersson, *Messianic Popular Movements in the Lower Congo,* London: Kegan Paul, 1958.

Georges Balandier, *Sociologie actuelle de l'Afrique noire. Dynamique des changements sociaux en Afrique centrale.* Paris: Presses Universitaires de France (1955), 1963.

J. Banda-Mwaka, 'Le Kimbanguisme en tant que mouvement prépolitique chez les Kongo', *Problèmes sociaux congolais* no. 92-93, March-June 1971, 3-53.

E. Bazola, 'Le Kimbanguisme', *Cahiers des religions africaines* 2/3, Jan. 1968, 144-152.

Willy Béguin and Marie-Louise Martin, 'Découverte du Kimbanguisme', in: *Le monde non-chrétien* 22/89-90, Jan.-July 1969, 5-37.

J. E. Bertsche, 'Kimbanguism: A Challenge to Missionary Statesmanship', *Practical Anthropology* 13/1, Jan.-Febr. 1966, 13-33.

Simon Boka and Paul Raymaekers, 250 *Chants de l'EJCSK. I. Première série: 85 chants de Nsambu André, Notes et Documents.* Kinshasa: Université Lovanium, 1960, no. 3.

D. Buana-Kibongi, 'L'évolution du Kimbanguisme', *Flambeau* no. 10, May 1966, 75-81.

W. P. Burton, *When God Changes a Man. A True Story of This Great Change in the Life of a Slave-Trader.* London: Victory Press, 1929.

— *God Working With Them, Being 18 years Congo Evangelistic Mission History.* London: Victory Press, 1933.

C. Carmichael, 'Congo', *Pentecostal Evangel* 2994, 26.9.1971, 19f.

M. J. Casebow, *Mvutu mu Kimbanguisme,* Ngombe-Lutete, 1958.

Catéchisme du Kintwadi (11.7.1957), French and Kikongo in: P. Raymaekers, *Zaïre* 13/7, 1959, 737-40.

Le Catéchisme concernant le prophète Simon Kimbangu. N'Kamba 1970.

Paul-Eric Chassard, 'Essai de bibliographie sur le Kimbanguisme', *Archives de Sociologie des Religions* 16/31, 1971, 43-49.

F. Choffat, 'L'église kimbanguiste africaine et non-violente', *Cahiers de la réconciliation* nos. 5-6, May-June 1966, 3-15.

Jules Chomé, *La passion de Simon Kimbangu.* Brussels: Présence Africaine, 1959.

C.R.I.S.P., Courrier Africain no. 47, 8.1.1960: Le Kimbanguisme.

R. P. Decapmaeker, 'Le Kimbanguisme', in: *Devant les sectes non-chrétiennes,* Rapports et compte rendu de la XXXIme semaine de *missiologie.* Louvain 1961, 52-90.

Dominique Desanti, 'The Golden Anniversary of Kimbanguism. An African Religion'. *Continent* 2000. *Africa's Bilingual Monthly,* No. 19, April 1971, 7-19.

K. S. Dialungana, *Ksikulusu za Dibundu.* N'Kamba: EJCSK, 1960.

— *Zolanga Yelusalemi dia Mpa.* N'Kamba: EJCSK, 1961.

— *Tanganinia Fu Ya Klisto.* N'Kamba: EJCSK, 1966.

Joseph Diangienda, 'Etablissement et organisation de l'église (Lusansu)' (22.6.1958), *C.R.I.S.P.* no. 47, 8.1.1960, 20f.
— 'Le Kimbanguisme', *C.R.I.S.P.* no. 49, 22.1.1960, 19f.
— 'Coup d'Oeil sur le Kimbanguisme', *Kimbanguisme* (Kinshasa), May 1960.
— 'Eglise et politique', *Cahiers de la réconciliation,* nos. 5-6, May-June 1966, 40-42.
La Documentation catholique, no. 1547, Sept. 1969, 830: L'Eglise Kimbanguiste admise au C.O.E.
A. Doutreloux, 'Prophétisme et "leadership" dans la société Kongo', in: *Devant les sectes non-chrétiennes,* XXXIe semaine de *missiologie,* Louvain, Museum Lessianum, 1961, no. 42, 67-81.
Ecumenical Review 19/1, Jan. 1967, 29-36.
H. W. Fehderau, 'Kimbanguism: Prophetic Christianity in Congo', *Practical Anthropology* 9/4, July-Aug. 1962, 157-178.
Charles-André Gilis, *Kimbangu, fondateur d'église.* Brussels: La Librairie encyclopédique, 1960.
J. Giraud, 'La Pentecôte au Congo', *Viens et Vois* 35/7-8, July-Aug. 1967, 22-23; 35/11, Nov. 1967, 24-25.
H. E. Heimer, 'Kimbanguists in the Congo', *World Call* (Indianapolis), March 1970, 16f.
W. J. Hollenweger, *Marxist and Kimbanguist Mission. A Comparison.* Birmingham: University of Birmingham, 1973.
C. Hoskyns, *The Congo Since Independence. January 1960—December 1961,* Oxford U.P., 1965.
R. Italiaander, 'Prophet und Märtyrer im Kongo. Wirksamkeit und Leiden des Simon Kimbangu', *Evangelisches Missions-Jahrbuch* 1970. Hamburg, 1970, 31-44.
Kare Juul (ed), *Til jordens ender. Norsk pinsemisjon gjennom 50 ar* Oslo: Filadelfiaforlaget, 1960.
Christian Krust, 'Die Kimbanguistenkirche im Kongo', *Heilszeugnisse* 55/10, 1.10.1970, 147f.
Jean Lasserre, 'L'Eglise kimbanguiste du Congo', in: *Le monde non-chrétien,* nos. 79-80, July-Dec. 1966, 45-52.
K. P. Luzolo, *Mvand'avelela mu Ntumwa Yisu.* N'Kamba: EJCSK, 1959.
Wyatt MacGaffey, 'The Beloved City: Commentary On a Kimbanguist Text', *Journal of Religion in Africa* 2/2, 1969, 129-147.
Marie-Louise Martin, *Kirche ohne Weisse. Simon Kimbangu und seine Millionenkirche im Kongo.* Basel: Reinhardt, 1971.
— 'Prophetism in the Congo. Origin and development of an

independent African church', *Ministry* 8/4, Oct. 1968, 154-163.
— *Prophetic Christianity in the Congo. The Church of Christ on Earth through the Prophet Simon Kimbangu.* Braamfontein/ Johannesburg: The Christian Institute of Southern Africa, no date (c. 1970).
— 'Afrikanische Gestalt des christlichen Glaubens: Die Kirche Jesu Christi auf Erden durch den Propheten Simon Kimbangu.' *Ev. Missionszeitschrift* 28/1, Jan. 1971, 16-29.
— 'Congolese Church Celebrates', *Pro Veritate* 10, 15.6.1971, 4f.
I. Masembo, *Le Prophétisme kongo.* Unpublished thèse de licence en théologie, 1966 (University of Strasbourg).
J. Masson, 'Simples réflexions sur les chants kimbanguistes', in: *Devant les sectes non-chrétiennes*, XXXIe semaine de missiologie, Louvain, Museum Lessianum, 1961, no. 42, 82-90.
R. G. Mitchell and H. W. Turner, *A Bibliography of Modern African Movements.* North-Western University Press. 1966 (Follow up in: *Journal of Religion in Africa* 1, 1968, 173-210).
M. W. Moorhead, *Missionary Pioneering in Congo Forest.* A narrative of the labours of William F. P. Burton and his companions in the native villages of Luba-Land, compiled from letters, diaries and articles, London: Assemblies of God Publ. House, no date.
F. M'Vuendy, *Le Kimbanguisme de la clandestinité à la tolérance* (1921-1959), Paris, Diplôme E.P.H.E., 1969 (unpublished).
G. Mwene-Batende, *Etude sociologique des conflits entre les Eglises congolaises. Cas particulier de quelques églises de souche kimbanguiste.* Kinshasa, Univ. Lovanium, Mémoire de licence en sociologie, 1970 (unpublished).
Nfinangani and Nzungu, *Histoire de Simon Kimbangu,* Prophète (1921). This is the earliest report, written by Kimbangu's secretaries. It was found in the archives of the 'Service Colonial des Affaires Indigènes et de la Main d'Oeuvre, Léopoldville' (today Kinshasa); printed in French in: *Archives de Sociologie des Religions* 16/31, 1971, 15-42.
Ngindu, 'Colloque sur le Kimbanguisme' (1972), *Revue du Clergé Africain* 27/6, Nov. 1972, 631-645.
O. Niederberger, 'Die Kimbangu-Kirche im Weltrat der Kirchen', *Neue Zeitschrift für Missionswissenschaft* 27/3, 1971, 215-19.
Nkanda Bisamu bia Simon Kimbangu (French sub-title: Office du prophète Simon Kimbangu), 1961.
B. N'tontolo, *Les mouvements prophétiques et les réveils*

126

spirituels dans le Bas-Congo. Brussels: Faculté libre de théol. protestante, 1968 (unpublished).

Paul Raymaekers, 'L'Eglise de Jésus-Christ sur la terre par le prophète Simon Kimbangu: contribution à l'étude des mouvements messianiques dans le Bas-Kongo', *Zaïre* 13/7, 1959, 675-756.

A. Ryckmans, *Les mouvements prophétiques kongo en* 1958. Contribution à l'étude de l'histoire Congo, Kinshasa, Bureau d'Organisation des Programmes Ruraux, 1970 (reprinted from N'Konge-Kongo, 1964, no. 7).

Martial Sinda, *Le messianisme congolais et ses incidences politiques. Kimbanguisme, matsouanisme, autres mouvements.* Paris: Payot, 1972.

Leonhard Steiner, 'Die Kimbanguistenkirche im Kongo', *Wort und Geist* 2/7, July 1970.

J. Vernaud, 'Congo', *Viens et Vois* 37/6, June 1969, 23f; 37/7-8, July-Aug. 1969, 20f; 36/10, Oct. 1968, 21f.

G. Wainwright, 'Theological Reflections on "The Catechism concerning the Prophet Simon Kimbangu" of 1970', *Orita, Ibadan Journal of Religious Studies* 6/1, June 1971, 22f.

R. Wikisi et al., 'Mise au point sur le Kimbanguisme', *C.R.I.S.P.,* no. 47, 8.1.1960, 18-20.

J. van Wing. 'Le Kibanguisme vu par un témoin', *Zaïre* 12/6, 1958, 563-618.

On Chapter IV: The Holy Spirit and the Virgin Mary

Sergio Mendez Arceo, 'La antorcha de la verdad', *La Voz* 1/1 (1966?), 18-20, 31.

Ernst Benz, *Der Heilige Geist in Amerika.* Düsseldorf: Diederichs, 1970.

Pamela M. Binyon, *The Concepts of 'Spirit' and 'Demon'. A Study in the use of different languages describing the same phenomena.* Unpublished M.A. Thesis, University of Birmingham, 1974.

Arnold Bittlinger. *Im Kraftfeld des Heiligen Geistes.* Marburg a.d.Lahn: Edel, 1968; English: *Gifts and Graces. A commentary on I Cor.* 12-14. London: Hodder & Stoughton, 1967.

— 'The Charismatic Worship Service in the New Testament and Today', *Studia Liturgica* 9/4, 1973, 215-229.

— 'Die Glossalie innerhalb der charismatischen Bewegung', *Materialdienst* (Stuttgart) 35/18, 15.9.1972, 275-279.

C. A. Bolten, 'The Recent Vatican Council', *Pent. Evangel* 2703, 27.2.1966, 6f.

Louis Bouyer, 'Charismatic Movements in History within the Church Tradition', *One in Christ* 10/2, 1974, 148-161.

James Byrne, *Threshold of God's Promise. An introduction to the Catholic Pentecostal Movement.* Notre Dame, Ind.: Ave Maria Press, 1970, 1971[3].

Henri Caffarel, *Faut-il parler d'un Pentecôtisme catholique?* Paris: Editions du Feu Nouveau, 1973.

Miriam Castiglione, *I neo-pentecostali in Italia (dal 'Jesus Movement' ai 'Bambini di Dio').* Torino: Claudiana, 1974.

Jim Cavnar, *Prayer Meetings.* Pecos, New Mexico: Dove Publ., and Watchung, N.J.: Charisma Books, 1969.

Stephen Clark, *Building Christian Communities. Strategy for Renewing the Church.* Notre Dame, Ind.: Ave Maria Press, 1972.

— *Confirmation and the 'Baptism of the Holy Spirit'.* Pecos, New Mexico: Dove Publ., 1969 and Watchung, N.J.: Charisma Books, 1971.

— *Spiritual Gifts.* Ibidem, 1969/71.

— *Baptized in the Spirit.* Ibidem, 1970/71.

Leone Cristiani, art. 'Pentecostali', *Enciclopedia Cattolica* IX (1952) 1153f.

Prudencio Damboriena, 'El protestantismo en Chile', *Mensaje* 6/59, June 1957, 145-154.

— 'Algunos aspectos de la penetración protestante en Iberoamerica', *Arbor* (Madrid) 50/192 (misprint 49/192), Dec. 1961, 60-75 (624-639).

— 'Pentecostal Fury', *Catholic World* 202/201, Jan. 1966.

— *Tongues as of Fire. Pentecostalism in Contemporary Christianity.* Washington and Cleveland: Corpus Books, 1969.

Max Delespesse, *The Church Community Leaven and Life Style.* Ottawa: The Catholic Centre of Saint Paul University, 1969; Notre Dame, Ind.: Communication Center, 1972.

Directory of Catholic Prayer Groups. Currently from: Center of Communication and Service, True House, 1255 E. Madison, South Bend, Ind. 46617.

Jean Duchesne, *Jesus Revolution Made in USA.* Paris: Le Cerf, 1972.

Mildred A. Duncan, *A Revelation of End-Time Babylon. A Verse by Verse Exposition of the Book of Revelation.* Edgemont, South Dakota: M. H. Duncan, 1950.

Reiner-Friedemann Edel (ed.), *Kirche und Charisma. Die Gaben des Heiligen Geistes im Neuen Testament, in der Kirchengeschichte und in der Gegenwart.* Marburg a.d.Lahn: Edel, 1966.

Expériences no. 8, 1972, 13-20: '90% des évêques des USA sont favorables au mouvement charismatique. L'un d'eux, l'évêque J. McKinney explique son expérience.'

Joseph Fiorentino, *The New Pentecost and the Old*. Woburn, Mass., author, 1971.

Balthasar Fischer, 'The Meaning of the Expression "Baptism in the Spirit" in the light of Catholic Baptismal Liturgy and Spirituality', *One in Christ* 10/2, 1974, 172f.

Josephine Massingberd Ford, 'Toward a Theology of "Speaking in Tongues",' *Theol. Studies* 32, 1971, 3-29.

— 'Pentecostal Catholicism', *Concilium* 9/8, Nov. 1972, 85-90.

— *Baptism of the Spirit. Three Essays on the Pentecostal Experience*. Techny, Ill.; Divine Word Publ., 1971.

— *The Pentecostal Experience. A New Direction for American Catholics*. London etc.: Paulist Press, 1970.

— *The Spirit and the Human Person. A Meditation*. Dayton, Ohio: Pflaum Press, 1969.

Arturo Gaëte, 'Un cas d'adaptation: Les "Pentecostales" au Chili', in: Abd-el-Jali, D. Rops, R. P. Houang, O. Lacombe, P.-H. Simon, *L'Eglise, l'occident, le monde*, Paris: Libr. Arthème Fayard (Recherches et Débats 15), 1956, 142-9.

Donald L. Gelpi, *Pentecostal Piety*. New York: Paulist Press, 1972.

David Geraets, *Baptism of Suffering*. Pecos, New Mexico: Dove Publ.; Watchung, N.J.: Charisma Books, 1970.

Bert Ghezzi, 'Just the Beginning', *Acts* 1/2, Sept.-Oct. 1967, 34.

— 'Mi mundo se ha enderazado', *La Voz* 4/4, 1969, 8f.

J. Giblet, 'Baptism in the Spirit in the Acts of the Apostles', *One in Christ* 10/2, 1974, 162-171.

Quentin Hakenwerth, *The Prayer of Faith*. St. Louis, Mo.,: Maryhurst Press, 1969.

— *The Grain of Wheat*. St. Louis, Mo.: Maryhurst Press, 1967.

Gotthold Hasenhüttl, *Charisma, Ordnungsprinzip der Kirche*. (Oekumenische Forschungen I/V). Freiburg: Herder, 1969.

Virginia H. Hine 'Pentecostal Glossolalia. Toward a Functional Interpretation', *Journal for the Scientific Study of Religion* 8/2, 1969, 211-226.

Walter J. Hollenweger, *New Wine in Old Wineskins. Protestant and Catholic Neo-Pentecostalism*. Gloucester: Fellowship Press, 1973.

An Introduction to the Catholic Charismatic Renewal. Notre Dame, Ind.: Communication Center, no date.

George J. Jennings, 'An Ethnological Study of Glossolalia',

Journal of the American Scientific Association, March 1968, 5-16.

Morton T. Kelsey, *Encounter with God. A Theology of Christian Experience*. Minneapolis, Minn.; Bethany Fellowship, Inc., 1972.

— *Tongue Speaking, An experiment in spiritual experience*. New York: Doubleday, 1964.

Francisco Lepargneur, 'Reflexoes católicas en face do Movimento Pentecostal no Brasil', in: Associaçao de Seminários Teológicos Evangélicos (ASTE), *O Espírito Santo e o Movimento Pentecostal*: Simpósio S. Paulo: ASTE, 1966, 47-67.

Ivar Lundgren, *Ny pingst. Rapport fran en nutida väckelse i gamla kyrkor*. Oslo: Den kristna bokringen, 1970.

Sandro Magister, 'La pentecoste dei poveri', *Sette Giorni* no. 304, 29.4.1973, 19-23.

— 'La febbre del sacro teatro', *ibidem* no. 305, 6.5.1973, 47-50.

George Martin, *Growing in the Spirit*. Pecos, New Mexico: Dove Publ., 1972.

Ralph Martin, *Unless the Lord Build the House . . . The Church and the New Pentecost*. Notre Dame, Ind.: Ave Maria Press, 1971.

— 'David Wilkerson's vision', *New Covenant* 3/6, Jan. 1974, 11f.

Jerome McCarthy, 'The Charismatic Renewal and Reconciliation in Northern Ireland?' *One in Christ* 10/1, Jan. 1974, 31-43.

— *The Significance of Neo-Pentecostalism for Ecumenism*. Unpubl. Thesis B.Phil., University of Hull, 1973.

Kilian McDonnell, 'The Ecumenical Significance of the Pentecostal Movement', *Worship* 40/10, Dec. 1966, 608-29.

— 'The Ideology of Pentecostal Conversion', *Journal of Ecumenical Studies* 5/1, Winter 1968, 105-126.

— 'Holy Spirit and Pentecostalism', *Commonweal* 89, 8.11.1968, 198-204.

— 'Catholic Pentecostalism. Problems in Evaluation', *Dialog*, Winter 1970, 35-54; reprint: Watchung. N.J.: Charisma Books, 1971.

— (together with A. Bittlinger). *The Baptism in the Holy Spirit as an Ecumenical Problem. Two Essays Relating the Baptism in the Holy Spirit to Sacramental Life*. Notre Dame, Ind.: Charismatic Renewal Services, 1972.

— 'The Experiential and the Social: New Models from Pentecostal/Roman Catholic Dialogue', *One in Christ* 9/1, 1973, 43-58.

— 'Catholic charismatics. The rediscovery of a hunger for

God and the sense of his presence', *Commonweal* 96/9, 1972, 207-211.

— 'Statement of the Theological Basis of the Catholic Charismatic Renewal', *One in Christ* 10/2, 1974, 206-215.

— 'The Distinguishing Characteristics of the Charismatic-Pentecostal Spirituality', *One in Christ* 10/2, 1974, 117-128.

George McLeod, 'He Will Renew the Earth', *New Covenant* 2/12, June 1973, 10-12.

Eugen Mederlet, 'Die Charismen in der römisch-katholischen Kirche heute' in: R. F. Edel (ed), *Kirche und Charisma*, 137-157.

Basil Meeking/John McTernan, 'The Roman Catholic-Pentecostal Diaologue', *One in Christ* 10/2, 1974, 106-110.

John Moore, 'The Catholic Pentecostal Movement', in: Michael Hill (ed): *A Sociological Yearbook of Religion in Britain* 6, 1973, 73-90.

Abdalazis de Moura, *Importância das Igrejas Pentecostais para a Igreja Católica*. Recife: duplicated, available from the author, Rua Jiriquiti 48, Boa Vista, Recife.

— 'O Pentecostalismo como fenômeno popular no Brasil', *Revista Eclesiástica Brasileira* 31/121, March 1971, 78-94.

Edward D. O'Connor, *The Laying on of Hands*. Pecos, New Mexico: Dove Publ. 1969 and Watchung, N.J.: Charisma Books, 1971.

— *The Pentecostal Movement in the Catholic Church*. Notre Dame, Ind.: Ave Maria Press, 1971.

— *Pentecost in the Catholic Church*. Pecos, New Mexico: Dove Publ. 1970; Watchung, N.J.: Charisma Books, 1971.

— *Pentecost in the Modern World. The Charismatic Renewal Compared With Other Trends in the Church and the World Today*. Notre Dame, Ind.: Ave Maria Press, 1972.

L. O'Docharty, 'I Tried to be a Good Catholic . . . ', *Testimony* 4/1, First Quarter 1965, 8.

Pentecostal Evangel 2860, 2.3.1969, 10: 'Priest Cites Growth of Pentecostalism', 2785, 24.9.1967, 6-7, 13: 'Pentecostal Meetings on Catholic Campuses', 3012, 30.1.1972, 27: ' "Eternity" Magazine Documents Catholic Renewal'; 3017, 5.3.1972, 15: 'Neo-Pentecostals Note Gain in Province of Quebec'; 3024, 24.4.1972, 27: 'Catholic Charismatic Conference Draws 1000'.

Vittorio Perres, 'I cattolici pentecostali', *Il Testimonio*, Nov.-Dec. 1973, 342-45.

David J. Du Plessis, *The Spirit Bade Me Go*. Plainfield, N.J.; Logos Int.; London: Fountain Trust, no date.

— 'David J. Du Plessis op het vaticaans concilie', *Vuur* 8/11, Jan. 1965, 12f.

— 'The Historic Background of Pentecostalism', *One in Christ* 10/2, 1974, 174-179.

— 'Persecution for Charismatic Catholics?' *New Covenant* 3/6, Jan. 1974, 13.

E. E. Plowman, 'Catholics Get the Spirit', *Christianity Today* 16.7.1971.

K. Ranaghan, *Catholic Pentecostals.* New York: Paulist Press, 1969.

— (ed), *As the Spirit Leads Us.* New York: Paulist Press, 1971.

David E. Rosage, *Retreats and the Catholic Charismatic Renewal.* Plainfield, N.J.: Logos Int.; Watchung, N.J.: Charisma Books; Pecos, New Mexico: Dove Publications, 1971.

William Samarin, *Tongues of Men and Angels. The Religious Language of Pentecostalism.* New York and London: Collier-Macmillan, 1970.

Michael Scanlan, *The Power in Penance. Confession and the Holy Spirit.* Notre Dame, Ind.: Ave Maria Press, 1972.

Wilhelm Schamoni, 'Die Charismen in der Geschichte der römisch-katholischen Kirche', in: R. F. Edel (ed), *Kirche und Charisma,* 88-107.

F. J. Schulgen, 'I Knew That Heaven Begins on Earth . . . ' *Testimony* 4/1, First Quarter 1965, 1-7.

John L. Sherrill, *They Speak With Other Tongues.* McGraw-Hill edition 1964.

Viviers 1973. *Rencontre Charismatique Interconfessionnelle,* 31.10-4.11.1973, no place, 1973.

La Voz 4/4, 1969, 28-31: 'Ecatólicos: El movimiento pentecostal en los Estados Unidos'.

R. Douglas Wead, *Catholic Charismatics. Are They For Real?* Carol Stream, Ill.: Creation House, 1973.

William J. Whalen, 'The Pentecostals', *U.S. Catholic* 32/10, Febr. 1967, 12-16.

J. Zeegers, 'Het volle Evangelie in de R. K. Kerk', *Pinksterboodschap* 3/4, April 1962, 13.

Josef Sudbrack, 'Im Spiegel der Zeit. Streiflichter des nordamerikanischen Christentums', *Geist und Leben* 43/5, Nov. 1970, 369-387.

Francis A. Sullivan, 'The Pentecostal Movement', *Gregorianum* 53/2, 1972, 238-65.

Emmanuel Sullivan, 'Can the Pentecostal Movement Renew the Churches?' *Study Encounter* 8/4, 1972.

Vinson Synan, *The Holiness-Pentecostal Movement in the United States*. Grand Rapids, Mich.: Wm. B. Eerdmans Publ. Co., 1971.

Willmar Thorkelson, 'They're Filled With the Spirit', *This Month* (WCC), no. 21, Aug. 1972, 3f.

Simon Tugwell, *Did You Receive the Spirit?* London: Darton, Longman & Todd, 1972.

— 'The Gift of Tongues in the New Testament', *Expository Times* 84/5, Febr. 1973, 137-140.

— 'Reflections on the Pentecostal Doctrine of "Baptism in the Holy Spirit', *Heythrop Journal* 13/3, July 1972, 268-281; 13/4, Oct. 1972, 402-414.

— *Catholic Pentecostalism. An Evaluation.* London: Catholic Truth Society, 1973.

Ignacio Vergara, 'Avance de los "Evangélicos" en Chile', *Mensaje* 3/41, Aug. 1955, 257-262.

— *El protestantismo en Chile.* Santiago de Chile: Editorial del Pacifico, 1962.

W. W. Verhoef, 'De reformatorische houdling jegens de rooms-katholieke kerk en haar leden', *Vuur* 6/5-6, July/Aug. 1962, 11-13.

On Chapter V: The Wisdom of the Children

Gerhard Adler, *Die Jesus-Bewegung. Düsseldorf,* Patmos-Verlag, 1972.

Helmut Aichelin, 'Das chemische Pfingsten. Droge und neue Religiosität'. *Information* no. 48, Nov. 1971 (Ev. Zentralstelle für Weltanschauungsfragen, Stuttgart).

— 'Children of God. Extremisten der Jesusbewegung', *Materialdienst* 35/23, 1.12.1972, 350-354; 35/24, 15.12.1972, 366-370.

— 'Die "Jesus-Revolution". Entwicklungen und Kriterien'. *Materialdienst* 35/1, 1.1.1972, 2-6.

Mother Basilea, *Thoughts About the Booklet 'The True Story of Moses and the Children of God',* dupl.

Yves A. Bebié, 'Auf der Jesuswelle', *Tagesanzeiger* (Zurich), 2.11.1971, 13.

— 'Rückfall in die naive Schriftgläubigkeit', *Tagesanzeiger Magazin,* 11.3.1972, 15.

— 'Auch in der Schweiz?', *Tagesanzeiger* 22.9.1971, 22.

Andreas Benda, *Heute mit Jesus.* Brunnen: Aussaat, 1973.

David Berg, *Letters From a Shepherd.* Dallas, Texas: Children of God, 1972.

— *Classes.* Dallas, Texas: Children of God, no date.

Revolution for Jesus. Basic Instructions. Dallas, Texas: Children of God, no date.

— *Survival.* The True Story of 'Moses' and the 'Children of God'. Dallas, Texas: Children of God, no date.

Virginia Brandt Berg, *The Promise of God are Streams That Never Run Dry.* Dallas, Texas: Children of God, no date.

— *The Hem of His Garment, or: From Deathbed to Pulpit Overnight.* Dallas, Texas: Children of God, no date.

Horst Klaus Berg, 'Interview—February 1972', *Ru*4, 1972.

— 'Die Religion der Jesus-People', *Katechetische Blätter* 97, 1972, 735-50.

Piero Bertolini and Laura Cavana, 'Il problema della droga e i giovani d'oggi', *Pedagogia e vita* 33, 1972, 565-580.

Arthur Blessitt with Walter Wagner, *Turned On to Jesus.* London: Word Books, 1972.

— *Tell the World-Techniques of Out-Reach Witnessing.* London: Lakeland, 1972.

Bruno Borchert, 'Jesus-Movement', *Concilium* 79, 1972, 101-105.

A. Broek, 'Jesus Movement: wordt Jezus de Man-van-het-jaar?' *Jeugden Samenleving* 2, 1972, 17-29.

— 'Nadere verantwoording. Een reaktie of het kommentar von Johanna Fortuin op het artikel Jesus Movement', *Jeugden samenleving* 2, 1972, 836-40.

Cam 26/1, 1972, 28: 'Agnew applauds Jesus movement in talk to Greek Orthodox'.

Willy Canziani, 'Sehnsucht nach dem grossen Glück', *Züri-Leu* (Zurich) 27.1.1972, 41.

John Capon, *And There Was Light. The story of the nation-wide festival of light.* Woking: Lutterworth Press, 1972.

Xavier de Chalendar, *Morto sotto Ponzi Pilato ma tuttora vivente.* Bari: Paoline, 1973.

Christsein '73. Junge Bewegungen berichten. Kassel: Rolf Kühne Verlag, 1972.

Bob Combs, *God's Turf.* Old Tappan, N.J.: F. H. Revell, 1969.

Geoffrey Corry, *Jesus Bubble or Jesus Revolution. The Growth of Jesus Communes in Britain and Ireland.* London: British Council of Churches, 1973.

Nicky Cruz *Gives the Facts on Drugs,* Plainfield, N.J.: Logos Int., 1971.

Sigurd Martin Daecke, 'Für und wider die Jesus People Bewegung', *Ev. Kommentare* 5, 1972, 155-158.

Dagen 18.5.1972 (Unge Kommunister gar över till Jesus), 28.4.1972 (Omvänd marxist talar pa möte mot marxismen),

13.5.1972 (Vi maste avslöja hotet mot vart lands frihet!),
23.5.1972 (Regeringen maste ingripa mot revolutionsplaner).

Flo Dobbie, *Land Aflame*. London: Hodder and Stoughton, 1972.

Jean Duchesne, *Jesus Revolution made in USA*. Paris: Le Cerf, 1972.

Dick Eastman, *Up With Jesus*. Grand Rapids; Baker Book House, 1971.

O. Eggenberger, 'Zur Auswirkung der Jesus-Bewegung in der Schweiz', *Kirchenblatt für die reformierte Schweiz* 128, 1972, 258-261; 275-278.

Ludwig Eisenlöffel, 'Die gläubigen Hippies und die Oeffentlichkeit,' *Der Leuchter* 22/11, Nov. 1971, 5f; reprint: *Wort und Geist* 4/1, Jan. 1972, 7-10.

Marlin Van Elderen, 'The "Jesus Freak": Some Thoughts on a Religious Phenomenon', *The Reformed Journal*, May-June 1971.

Jerome Ellison, *God on Broadway*. Richmond, Va.: John Knox, 1971.

Robert Ellwood, *One Way*. Englewood Cliffs, N.J.: Prentice-Hall, 1973.

Roland M. Enroth, Edward E. Ericson, C. Breckinridge Peters, *The Jesus People. Old-Time Religion in the Age of Aquarius*. Grand Rapids, Mich.,: W. B. Eerdmans Publ., 1972; under the title *The Story of the Jesus People. A Factual Survey* published by Paternoster Press, Exeter.

Eulenspiegel, April 1972 (GDR): '1972 Jahre nach Christi Geburt'.

Clay Ford, *Berkely Journal. Jesus and the Street People. A Firsthand Report*. New York: Harper, 1972.

K. P. Frampton, *Beware—'The Children of God'*. London, Bromley, Kent (5 London Road), no date.

Hans Jürgen Geppert, *Wir Gotteskinder. Die Jesus-People Bewegung*. Gütersloh: Gerd Mohn, 1972.

Giovanni Gozzer, 'Superstar. Un mistero sacro moderno', *Humanitas* 27, 1972, 278-299.

Billy Graham, *The Jesus Generation*. London: Hodder and Stoughton, 1971.

Andrew M. Greeley, 'The New American Religion', *Concilium* 9/7, Nov. 1971, 111-123.

Darrell L. Guder, 'Die Jesus People begegnen der Kirche', *Ev. Kommentare* 5/1, Jan. 1972, 24-26.

G. C. de Haas, *Van Jongelingsvereniging tot Jesus People*. Kampen: J. H. Kok, 1972.

Jerry Halliday, *Spaced Out and Gathered In*, Old Tappan: F. H. Revell, 1972.

Jan Rainer Hermanns, *Kennst Du Jesus? Sozialreport über Jesus-Leute in Deutschland*. Munich: Kösel Verlag, 1972.

C. H. Hermansson, *Marxism och kristendom*. Stockholm 1972.

Albert v. d. Heuvel, 'The Jesus People: An Ecumenical Challenge', *This Month* (WCC, Geneva), Febr. 1972, 3-5; reprints in *Risk* 1972/1, 16-20 and in *Brethren Life and Thought* 17/3, 1972, 185f.

Holger Hoffmann, *Gott im Underground. Die religiöse Dimension der Popkultur*. Hamburg: Furche-Verlag, 1972.

Reinhold Iblacker, 'Randbemerkung zur Jesusbewegung', *Orientierung* 36, 1972, 215-217.

Isaiah, 'Special Interview with Willem Schot, WCC', *New Nation News* 5/7, 16.4.1973, 4f.

Michael Jacob, *Pop Goes Jesus. An investigation of pop religion in Britain and America*. London: Mowbrays, 1972.

Jesus People Report, Atlanta: Home Missions Board, SBC, 1972.

Curt Jonasson, 'Pingströrelsens inte enig om kommunistoffensiven', *Svenska Dagbladet* 15.5.1972.

Nicko Jonzon, *Fran narkotika till Kristus*. Stockholm 1970.

Erling T. Jorstad, *That New-Time Religion. The Jesus Revival in America*. Minneapolis, Minn.: Augsburg Publ. House, 1972.

Manfred Josuttis, Hanscarl Leuner et al., *Religion und die Droge. Ein Symposion über religiöse Erfahrungen unter Einfluss von Haluzinogenen*. Stuttgart: W. Kohlhammer, 1972.

Karl Kilsmo, *Marxist-Leninismens kamp mot kristen tro*. Orebro 1972.

Pat King, *The Jesus People Are Coming*. Watchung, N.J.: Charisma Books; Plainfield, N.J.: Logos Int., 1971.

Günther Klempnauer, *Christentum ist Brandstiftung. Die Jesus People im Kreuzfeuer*. Wuppertal: R. Brockhaus, 1972.

Walter L. Knight (comp.), *Jesus People Come Alive*. London: Coverdale House, 1972.

Wilfried Kroll (ed), *Jesus kommt! Report der 'Jesus Revolution' unter Hippies und Studenten in USA and anderswo*. Wuppertal: Aussaat. 1971.

— *Jesus Generation auch in Europa? Die Jesus-Revolution von Finnland bis Marokko*. Wuppertal: Aussaat, 1972.

Kathryn Kuhlman, *I Believe in Miracles*. Englewood Cliffs, N.J.: Prentice-Hall, Inc., 1969[13].

Hal Lindsay, *The Late Great Planet Earth*. Grand Rapids, Mich.: Zondervan Publ. House, 1971ff.

Manfred Linz, 'Eine religiöse Gegenkultur. Jesus-People und ihr Echo', *Lutherische Monatshefte* 1972, 105-107.

Wolf von Lojewski (ed), *Jesus People oder die Religion der Kinder*. Munich: Claudius Verlag, 1972.

Anne Lombard, *Le mouvement hippie aux Etats-Unis. Une double aliénation entre le rêve et la réalité, le salut et la perte.* Tournai: Casterman, 1972.

Martin Lönnebo and Anders Bejbom, *Väckelse—nu!* Stockholm; Verbum, 1972.

Ivar Lundgren, *Ny pingst. Rapport fran en nutida väckelse i gamla kyrkor.* Den kristna bokringen, 1972.

John MacDonald, *The House of Acts.* Carol Stream, Ill.: Creation House, Inc., 1972.

Eric Mayer, 'The Jesus People and the Churches', *Renewal* no. 36, Dec. 1971/Jan. 1972, 2-8.

Wulf Metz, 'Jesuswelle', *Lutherische Monatshefte* 1972/3, 150.

— 'Wie ich glühe, glüht ihr. Children of God, religiöser Wildwuchs im Vormarsch', *Lutherische Monatshefte* 13/2, Febr. 1974, 61-65.

Jess C. Moody, *The Jesus Freaks.* Waco: Word Books, 1971.

Hans Joachim Mund, 'Jesus People, amerikanische Modewelle oder geistliche Erweckung', *Theologische Revue* 68, 1972, 269-278.

New Nation News 5/7, 16.4.1973, 8: 'Our Family in Geneva'.

Ruben Ortega (comp.), *The Jesus People Speak Out! What do they really Believe?* London: Hodder & Stoughton, 1972.

Richard N. Ostling, 'The Jesus People Revisited', *Ecumenical Review* 63/250, April 1974, 232-242.

Paul V, 'Homélie, 26.3.1972, Les Jeunes et Jésus', *Documentation catholique* 69, 1972, 360f.

Bob Owen with Duane Pederson, *Jesus is alive and well. The truth behind the stickers and slogans.* London: Lutterworth, 1972.

Pentecostal Evangel 2979, 13.6.1971, 27 (1000 'Jesus People' Baptized in Ocean Off California), 2983, 20.6.1971, 27 (Graham favors Jesus people, but sees need of Bible study), 2988, 15.8.1971 (Few blacks seen in Jesus movement), 2990, 29.8.1971 (Jesus movement is more than fad), 2987, 8.8.1971, 25 (David Wilkerson writes maturity manual for Jesus people), 3011, 23.1.1972 ('Jesus people' seminar draws crowds to Protestant and Catholic churches), 3020, 26.3.1972, 25 (Jesus People returning to established churches), 3019, 19.3.1972, 25 ('Jews for Jesus' leader cites reason why Jewish youth turn to Christ), 3025, 30.4.1972 (University professor studies influence of Jesus Movement on college campuses).

Hans Joachim Petsch, *Religion aus dem Underground. Eine Anfrage an die Kirchen.* Freiburg (Switzerland): Imba Verlag, 1972.

David J. Du Plessis, 'Holy Spirit in Ecumenical Movement', in: Norris L. Wogen (ed), *Jesus, Where Are You Taking Us? Messages From the First International Lutheran Conference on the Holy Spirit.* Carol Stream, Ill.: Creation House, 1973, 223-250.

Edward E. Plowman, *The Jesus Movement in America. Accounts of Christian Revolutionaries in Action.* London: Hodder & Stoughton, 1971 (USA edition: *The Underground Church,* Elgin, Ill.: D. C. Cook Publ. Co.).

Wilhelm Quenzer, 'Ursachen und Phänomenologie einer Bewegung', *Information* no. 50 (Ev. Zentralstelle für Weltanschauungsfragen) III/72, 12-22.

Ramparts, Aug. 1971, 18: 'Jesus Now: Hogwash and Holy Water'.

James Rayne, 'Strong Delusions (2 Thess. 2: 11)', *The Reformation Review* 30, 1973, 78-113.

Rüdiger Reitz, 'Jesus befiehl, wir folgen! Was steht hinter dem Glauben der Jesus-people?' *Oekumenische Rundschau* 21/3, 1972, 370-77.

Renewal no. 38, April/May 1972, 7: 'The Children of God in the News'.

John J. Ryan, *The Jesus People. The Catholic Faith for Young Christians of Today.* London: Sheed and Ward, 1972.

Siegfried Scharrer, 'Integration des Gefühls in die Erfahrung des Glaubens', *Informationsbrief* no. 50 (Ev. Zentralstelle für Weltanschauungsfragen) III/72, 23-31.

Hannelore Schilling, 'Schlüssel zu neuen Welten. Droge und Esoterik', *Informationsbrief* no. 49 (Stuttgart).

Rudolf Schnackenburg, Joachim Lange, Gerhard Lohfink, Erich Zenger, *Jesus: Anfrage an uns.* Würzburg: Echter Verlag, 1971[2].

Anton Schulte, *Die Jesusbewegung in USA. Ein persönlicher Reisebericht.* Reinkamp-Baerl: Brendow, no date.

William L. Shirer, 'The Rise and Fall of the Fourth Reich', *New Nation News* 5/7, 16.4.1973, 6.

Stanley Sjöberg, 'Blodig revolution eller andlig väckelsen', *Dagen* 27.4.1972.

— 'Vi kämpar vidara i kärlek', *Dagen* 20.5.1972.

Chuck Smith, *The Reproducers. New Life for Thousands.* Glendale, Calif.: Regal Books, 1972.

Spiegel 26/8, 14.2.1972, 110-123: 'Jesus im Schaugeschäft'.

Volkhard Spitzer, 'Jesus People—Selbstdarstellung einer Gruppe', *Information* no. 50 (Ev. Zentralstelle für Weltanschauungsfragen) III/72, 2-11.

Albert Springer, 'Die Jesusbewegung', *Judenchristliche Gemeinde* no. 424, Febr. 1972, 2-10.

The Street People. Selections from 'Right ON!' Berkeley's Christian Underground Student Newspaper. London: Hodder & Stoughton; Valley Forge, Pa: Judson Press, 1971.

Jeannette Struchen, *Zapped By Jesus.* New York: J. B. Lippincott, 1972.

Erland Sundström, *Den karismatiska vagen.* Stockholm: Gummessons, 1971.

Johannes Vaerge, 'Med Jesus i hjertet. En tolkning af Jesus-bevaegelsen', *Kirche og Kultur* 78/7, 1973, 398-414.

John J. Vincent, *The Jesus Thing.* London: Epworth Press, 1973.

Hiley H. Ward, *The Far-Out Saints of the Jesus Communes. A First-hand Report and Interpretation of the Jesus People Movement,* New York: Association Press, 1972.

Leslie Watkins, *Collection of Articles in 'The Daily Mail', under the title 'The New Believers'.* Off-print, no date, no place.

David Wilkerson, 'The Jesus Revolution', *Pent. Evangel* 2987, 8.8.1971, 2f., 22.

Don Williams, *Call to the Streets.* Minneapolis, Minn.: Augsburg Publ. House, 1972.

Sherwood Eliot Wirt. *Jesus Power.* New York: Harper & Row, 1972.

Hildegunde Wöller, *Die getaufte Revolution. Mythus aus dem Underground.* Munich: Kaiser-Verlag, 1973.

Marie Zimmermann, *Jesus Movement. International bibliography 1972, indexed by computer.* Strasbourg, University, 1973 (RIC Supplément 4).

Index